Contents

The most beautiful thing we can experience
is the mysterious. It is the source of all true
art and science.

— Albert Einstein

1. The Journey Begins: Unraveling the Mystiques of Tachyons

As we stand at the frontier of scientific possibilities, one question propels itself into the minds of both casual science enthusiasts and dedicated physicists alike: is travel into the future not only plausible, but already occurring on a scale infinitesimally beyond our perception? The notion of tachyons - hypothetical particles that travel faster than light - offers an intoxicating glimpse into the nature of existence, igniting debates that span generations, challenging our understanding of time itself.

In "Tachyon Time Travel: Debunking Misconceptions About Superluminal Particles," we embark on a methodical exploration of this speculative frontier, working diligently to separate romantic myth from scientific plausibility. You'll walk alongside renowned physicists whose theoretical frameworks hold the key to untangling the cosmic mysteries of tachyons and their implications on time travel beyond simple fiction.

Our journey through this book will be one of curiosity grounded by evidence, using logic and reasoning to unlock the gates of innovation previously defined only by imagination. Join me, and together we'll navigate the rich tapestry of ideas surrounding tachyon dynamics as we embark on this mind-expanding odyssey into realms of speed unimaginable by the laws that currently govern our universe. Buckle up for an intellectual expedition that promises not just answers, but fresh perspectives on time and beyond.

2. The Concept of Tachyons: Beyond the Speed of Light

2.1. Understanding Superluminal Motion

To understand superluminal motion, we must first grapple with the fundamental principles of physics that govern particle behavior and the constraints imposed by the speed of light. Traditionally, the cosmic speed limit, established by Einstein's theory of relativity, postulates that nothing can exceed the speed of light in a vacuum, set at approximately 299,792 kilometers per second. However, the concept of tachyons introduces a radical alternative that challenges this very axiom.

Tachyons, as theorized particles, possess the intrinsic ability to move faster than light. Their existence hinges on the parameters of theoretical physics that allow for a state of being where traditional physical laws may not necessarily apply. Unlike ordinary particles, tachyons are imagined to have imaginary mass, a concept that deviates from the familiar tangible world yet is mathematically consistent within specific theoretical frameworks. Their properties suggest that they would lose energy as their speeds increase, implying that any tachyon perpetually moving at superluminal speeds would be perpetually "cold." This notion frames tachyons in a unique disciplinary context, one that encompasses not only physics but also philosophy, where the implications of speed and existence intertwine intricately.

To fully grasp superluminal motion, it is crucial to delve into the Lorentz transformations, which underpin Einstein's relativity. These transformations help define how time and space are interwoven and how they react as objects approach the speed of light. As these velocities grow closer to light speed, time dilates, and the length contracts according to the relative motion of the observer. Tachyons, however, are theorized to exist outside this framework in a realm where these laws do not forcibly apply. They would experience a counterintuitive reality: as their velocity increased beyond light speed, they could theoretically traverse distances instantaneously from one point to another in a way that conventional physics cannot encode.

Moreover, exploring the implications of superluminal particles must include considerations of causality, the chain of cause and effect that underpins much of our current understanding of both physics and metaphysics. Tachyons threaten this understanding because their superluminal velocities could lead to scenarios where effects precede their causes when viewed from certain frames of reference. Such paradoxes echo the complexities often nestled within discussions of time travel and temporal mechanics, beckoning curious minds to question not only the nature of speed but its impact on the fabric of reality itself.

In quantum mechanics, the dialogue surrounding superluminal motion continues. Understanding tachyons requires examining phenomena such as quantum entanglement, where particles seem to communicate instantaneously regardless of distance, an occurrence that might suggest a path towards reconciling faster-than-light interactions. If tachyons were to exist, they may resemble and even provide a foundational understanding for some of these entangled behaviors, offering insight into realms beyond our current theoretical grasp.

As we explore tachyons further, it becomes apparent that the implications extend into various scientific, philosophical, and even practical domains. The prospect of superluminal communication using tachyonic signals promises to revolutionize the way information is transmitted across vast cosmic distances, allowing for instantaneous communication that surpasses the limitations of light speed. Such developments could underpin networks that facilitate a broader understanding of our universe.

In conclusion, understanding superluminal motion invites us to reconfigure our comprehension of time, speed, and the very nature of existence. Tachyons, while remain hypothetical, symbolize both a frontier of scientific inquiry and a challenge to our deepest philosophical doctrines. They compel us to rethink the definitions of reality, where traditional barriers present a riddle to be solved through a blend of profound inquiry and rigorous scientific examination. As we navigate this intellectual landscape, the pursuit of understanding tachyons and their potential will continue to provoke discussions that traverse the realms of both science and philosophy, igniting imaginations as we seek to unlock the mysteries woven into the universe's fabric. Embracing both skepticism and curiosity, we embark on a journey that holds the promise of discovering not only superluminal particles but possibly, a deeper comprehension of our own existence.

2.2. Theoretical Models and Historical Context

The exploration of tachyons and their theoretical implications begins by tracing the historical context within which these concepts emerged. At their essence, tachyons symbolize humanity's relentless pursuit of knowledge and its quest to understand the universe.

The roots of the tachyon theory can be traced back to the early 20th century, a time when the frameworks of modern physics were being solidified. The advent of Einstein's theory of relativity fundamentally redefined concepts like speed, time, and causality, leading physicists to explore realms they had previously not considered. Before discussing the specific birth of tachyon concepts, we must establish the foundational principles encountered during this scientific revolution.

In the years leading to Einstein's formulation of the special theory of relativity in 1905, the prevailing notion was that light represented an absolute speed limit, one that could not be exceeded by any massive object. This concept emerged from the classical understanding of motion, primarily revolving around Newtonian mechanics, which dominated scientific thought for centuries. However, as scientists began to delve deeper, experimental evidence, particularly from the work on electromagnetism, demanded a reevaluation of these classical concepts.

It was in this fertile intellectual soil that ideas surrounding hypothetical particles began to take root. The seminal papers of physicists such as Hermann Minkowski and others transformed the abstract mathematical constructs of spacetime, intertwining the dimensions of space and time into a cohesive framework. Minkowski, a crucial figure, introduced the concept of four-dimensional spacetime, which would later be instrumental in the discussions surrounding tachyons. In this view, faster-than-light particles could theoretically exist if the structure of spacetime allowed for such alternatives to conventional motion.

The notion of particles traveling faster than light, however, did not gain immediate traction. It wasn't until the 1960s that serious research into tachyons emerged in mainstream physics. The theoretical formulations by Gerald Feinberg in 1967, which coined the term "tachyon," presented robust mathematical foundations for these hypothetical particles. Feinberg proposed that tachyons could hold imaginary mass, a radical departure from the established understanding of mass and energy. The idea suggested that as tachyons gained energy, rather than approaching a limiting velocity, they would move faster, theoretically defying conventional laws of causality and leading to counterintuitive scenarios.

While tachyons were birthed in the realm of theoretical speculation, their implications urged greater inquiry into the properties of particles and the behavior of the universe. Theoretical physicists began to explore how these particles could engage with the existing models of quantum field theory and relativity. This exploration was not merely academic; it was fueled by a desire to understand phenomena like dark matter and dark energy, where established particles fell short of explaining cosmic mystery.

Historical context underscores an ongoing dialogue between science and philosophy. As physicists navigated concepts of tachyons, they were unwittingly engaging with philosophical inquiries about the nature of reality, causality, and time itself. The idea that an entity could exist and behave in ways that challenged the intuitions prompted deep philosophical questions: What does it mean to move through time? Can causality be violated? If superluminal travel is possible, what are the constraints that govern not only particles but the very fabric of reality?

Moreover, the historical lens offers insights into broader scientific paradigms that impacted tachyon discourse. The rise of quantum mechanics introduced novel uncertainties and complexities to the dialogue around fundamental particles, with quantum entanglement and the superposition principle inviting playful yet rigorous speculations about particles that might exist beyond the constraints of spacetime. This interplay laid the groundwork for speculative overlaps between quantum mechanics and tachyon theory.

Integrating the insights from previous frameworks of inquiry, one can see that tachyon research reflects the wider scientific zeitgeist. It captures a penchant for pushing the boundaries of what is possible while remaining tethered to the rigorous standards of mathematical and experimental physics. The continuing journey of tachyon research symbolizes an intersection where historical context, theoretical models, and philosophical investigation galvanize together, shedding light on some of the universe's most profound mysteries and igniting ongoing fascination and debate within scientific circles and beyond.

As we navigate through the journey of exploring tachyons, we should appreciate how each new development, from early hypotheses to the marriage of quantum mechanics with relativity, has refined our understanding of existence and prompted us to reconsider time, causality, and the cosmos itself. Moving forward, these theoretical models will continue to enrich our comprehension of the universe and challenge the conventions that have long governed our scientific understanding. This exploration does not merely stop at tachyons but beckons toward an expansive dialogue across multiple disciplines, urging humanity to question the very essence of speed, time, and existence.

2.3. Einstein's Relativity and Tachyons

Einstein's theories, particularly his special theory of relativity, represent foundational pillars in modern physics that deeply influence our understanding of motion, time, and causality. These concepts provide crucial insights into the speculative framework surrounding tachyons, the hypothetical particles that are theorized to travel faster than light. To embark on this exploration, one must first grasp how relativity recalibrates conventional views of speed and the limitations it imposes.

At the heart of special relativity is the postulate that the speed of light is constant and serves as a cosmic speed limit. According to Einstein, as an object accelerates towards this limit, its mass effectively increases due to relativistic effects, requiring more and more energy to continue its acceleration. This creates a scenario where no object with mass can reach, let alone exceed, the speed of light. However, the existence of tachyons introduces a profound challenge to this concept. Unlike ordinary particles, tachyons are theorized to possess an "imaginary mass," which enables them to travel at superluminal speeds. This characteristic alters the dynamics of energy and momentum, suggesting a framework where increasing speed results not in infinite mass but rather in decreased energy. Consequently, a tachyon could be seen as perpetually moving at a velocity greater than that of light, an idea that diverges significantly from established physics.

Exploring the implications of tachyons within the construct of relativity invites an examination of causality—a principle stating that causes precede their effects. This notion becomes precarious with tachyons, as their ability to move faster than light could result in situations where an effect might be observed before its cause when viewed from particular frames of reference. Such scenarios generate tantalizing paradoxes, known as "causal loops," that challenge the linear perception of time and provoke debates within both physics and philosophy. Einstein's equations, particularly the Lorentz transformations, suggest that the very fabric of spacetime might accommodate such phenomena; however, the question then arises: what consequences would this have for our understanding of reality itself?

Diving deeper into the mathematical foundations laid by Einstein elucidates the analytical language through which our understanding of tachyons evolves. While Einstein's theories primarily address massive particles, the extension of these ideas into the realm of massless or hypothetical particles sets the stage for more abstract considerations. In his equations, the concept of spacetime becomes a four-dimensional canvas, where distances and intervals are measured differently relative to the observer's frame of reference. Tachyons, operating in this mathematical landscape, challenge our interpretation of distance and time—forcing a reevaluation of how events unfold and are perceived.

Moreover, implications of tachyons extend beyond theoretical narratives into practical inquiries. If the existence of tachyons were to be substantiated, the potential for superluminal communication could revolutionize how information is relayed across cosmic distances. Within this speculative context, tachyons may offer a unique conduit that enables messages to traverse gaps that would otherwise remain insurmountable given the constraints of light-speed communication. In a universe filled with vast spatial voids, such a capability would provide a remarkable benefit to gaining insights into distant cosmic events.

The dialogue surrounding tachyons often overlaps with discussions in quantum mechanics, where entangled particles exhibit instantaneous correlations, regardless of the distance separating them. Such phenomena hint at the possibility of superluminal influences. If tachyons exist, they could illuminate underlying connections between distant particles, contributing to a broader understanding of entanglement and instantaneous communication across the universe.

In summary, examining the intricacies of Einstein's relativity in conjunction with the proposal of tachyons reveals an exhilarating frontier at the intersection of fundamental physics and the very nature of time. While tachyons challenge the dogmas established by relativistic physics, they simultaneously offer rich avenues for exploration—bridging theoretical inquiry with philosophical ponderings, prompting humanity to reconsider the nature of speed, time, and existence itself. As we unravel the enigmatic tapestry of tachyon dynamics, the quest to understand these hypothetical particles becomes not only a pursuit of scientific knowledge but a reflection of our deepest curiosities about the cosmos we inhabit. The journey through which we explore these themes promises to enrich our perspectives, suggesting that perhaps hidden within the fabric of reality, there lies a realm where the constraints of time and speed are mere illusions awaiting revelation.

2.4. The Mathematical Foundations of Tachyons

The exploration of tachyons, or hypothetical particles that purportedly travel faster than light, fundamentally rests upon a bedrock of complex mathematics that extends from and enriches the understanding of relativistic physics. To comprehend how tachyons fit into the fabric of theoretical physics, we must delve into a series of mathematical principles and frameworks that illuminate their properties, behaviors, and implications. This discourse not only unpacks the equations that define tachyon motion but also situates these particles within the broader context of modern physics, challenging traditional notions of speed, time, and causality.

The mathematical underpinnings of tachyon dynamics originate from the principles laid out in special relativity. At the core of this theory are the Lorentz transformations, which enable physicists to describe how measurements of time and distance vary for observers in different inertial frames. These transformations reveal that as particles with real mass approach the speed of light, their relativistic mass increases and thus requires infinite energy to reach the speed of light itself. However, tachyons disrupt this paradigm by introducing the concept of imaginary mass represented mathematically as "$m^2 < 0$." Here, rather than experiencing an infinite increase in mass, they possess the unique property of increasing their velocities as their energy decreases.

Mathematically, the relationship between energy, momentum, and mass for tachyons can be expressed in terms of their respective equations originating from relativistic principles. In conventional terms, the energy of a particle is given by $E^2 = (pc)^2 + (mc^2)^2$, where

E is energy, p is momentum, m is mass, and c is the speed of light. For tachyons, substituting imaginary mass into the equation highlights the unconventional behavior of these particles, leading to the interpretation that they would exist on a hyperbolic trajectory in spacetime, resulting in behaviors that defy conventional structure.

By adopting a framework of complex analysis, we can further investigate the implications of tachyon existence. This approach invites consideration of complex numbers—a mathematical construct that extends beyond the real number system—suggesting that tachyonic equations may possess solutions that manifest physically in unexpected ways. The concept of a tachyon's "imaginary" characteristics aligns with this viewpoint, as applying complex numbers can lead to solutions that suggest non-causal influences across spacetime. As a result, the mathematics behind tachyons beckons a rigorous examination of how imaginary dimensions, when extended into real variables, could manifest into observable phenomena—albeit ones that strain credulity under our current scientific lens.

Continuing on this path, the mathematical formalism of quantum field theory (QFT) provides additional layers of understanding. In this domain, the idea of fields as fundamental entities through which particles interact necessitates a reevaluation of tachyon interactions within the quantum realm. Theoretical frameworks posit that tachyons would modify established interactions, where the existence of faster-than-light particles could lead to instabilities within the field dynamics. The massless or imaginary mass attribute of tachyons introduces the possibility of spontaneous symmetry breaking—a concept where fields can acquire mass through non-standard interactions. This proposition not only suggests a reevaluation of mass generation processes observed within particle physics but also illuminates pathways for exploring underlying quantum behaviors that may arise from tachyonic influences.

As we reconcile these mathematical abstractions with physical realities, we consider their implications for causality and temporal mechanics. The introduction of tachyons could lead to phenomena such as retrocausality, where effects precede their causes due to the hyperbolic traversal of spacetime. This compelling narrative is mathematically supported within certain frameworks, hinting at the logical structures that sustain causal loops. By manipulating the mathematical language of spacetime within which tachyons reside, we confront challenging questions about the nature of time itself, thereby impacting both theoretical frameworks and philosophical discourse.

Explore the contemporary implications of tachyon theory leads to a profound consideration of their role in cosmological contexts. If tachyons exist, their ability to influence spacetime expansion could offer insights into dark matter and dark energy—enigmatic components that constitute a fundamental part of the universe yet resist conventional explanatory frameworks. Integrating tachyonic considerations into cosmological models may yield fresh approaches to understanding gravitational phenomena at cosmological scales, where particles traverse vast distances and interrelations speedily.

In light of these explorations, it becomes evident that the mathematical foundations of tachyons encapsulate a rich tapestry of knowledge that extends across multiple disciplines. Their analysis, rooted in both relativity and quantum mechanics, fosters a deeper awareness of the universe, elevating the discourse from abstract theorization to a robust engagement with the nature of existence itself. The continued study of tachyons encourages scientific inquiry to push the boundaries of knowledge, prompting new methodologies and futuristic paradigms that redefine our ascertainment of speed and time, ultimately positioning tachyons as a compelling frontier in modern physics. In this journey through mathematics, we glimpse not only hypothetical particles but a potential rethinking of cosmic scales and our very perception of reality itself.

2.5. Debunking Popular Myths

To navigate the idea of tachyons and their implications effectively, we must first address several myths that have arisen from both public fascination and misinterpretation of scientific principles. These myths range from overly simplistic understandings of tachyon travel to deeper misconceptions about the underlying physics governing their behavior and existence.

One of the most pervasive myths is the idea that tachyons, if they exist, would allow instantaneous travel or communication across cosmic distances. This stems from the misconception that superluminal particles operate outside the laws of physics as we know them, leading to the assumption that they can bypass time altogether. In reality, tachyons, although theorized to travel faster than light, would still be bound by the constraints imposed by relativity. The implications of faster-than-light behavior do not equate to instantaneous transport or communication. Rather, tachyons would complicate our understanding of causality, opening a Pandora's box filled with paradoxes that challenge linear notions of time.

Another common misunderstanding revolves around the concept of imaginary mass. While it is true that tachyons are hypothesized to possess imaginary mass, many misconstrue this to mean that such particles have no mass or weight in a conventional sense. This interpretation leads to the assumption that tachyons could be manipulated or created with ease, further fostering the dream of practical applications such as time travel machines or superluminal communications devices. However, an imaginary mass does not imply a lack of physicality or existence; rather, it signifies a unique and complex interaction with spacetime that defies traditional models of particle behavior.

Moreover, the myth that tachyons violate the principles of causality deserves careful scrutiny. Critics often claim that if tachyons were real, they would enable effects to precede causes, leading to logical contradictions and paradoxes often dramatized in science fiction narratives. While it is true that tachyons could theoretically produce these scenarios, the existence of tachyons does not automatically imply a breakdown of causality. In many proposed models, these faster-than-light particles are understood within a coherent framework that formally accommodates causality, while still offering complex interactions that provoke deeper philosophical questions about the nature of time itself.

Similarly, the notion that tachyons contradict Einstein's relativity is misleading. In fact, many theoretical models proposing tachyonic behavior arise as extensions of relativistic principles rather than critiques of them. While relativity asserts that nothing with real mass can travel faster than light, tachyons emerge from a conceptual space wherein traditional definitions of mass and energy dynamics are transformed. To argue that tachyons invalidate relativity distracts from the nuances of these discussions.

Another myth centers on the supposed ease of detecting tachyons or creating them in laboratory environments. Given their hypothetical nature, there is no experimental evidence to suggest that tachyons can be isolated or observed directly, nor has any experiment yielded conclusive results that support their existence. The idea that scientists might soon discover or prove tachyons often overlooks the rigorous validation processes fundamental to scientific inquiry. As promising as tachyon theories may be, real-world validation is a demanding labyrinth of experimental design, analysis, and publication that takes time, resources, and often, decades of work.

Beyond misconception, a significant number of enthusiasts within the speculative community embrace tachyons as a tantalizing solution to longstanding scientific mysteries, such as the nature of dark matter or dark energy. While the allure of a theoretical particle that could explain complex cosmological phenomena is appealing, this notion often simplifies intricate scientific problems into oversimplified narratives. It is essential to approach tachyons as part of a broader tapestry of open questions in physics rather than as miracle keys that unlock every mystery of the universe.

Finally, the myth that tachyons are mere science fiction constructs negates the depth of exploration and inquiry that has gone into this concept over the decades. While it is undeniable that popular media have played significant roles in shaping discussions around tachyons, the scientific community has undertaken rigorous theoretical pursuits and debates surrounding superluminal particles' potential and implications. Such discussions intersect with historical developments and philosophical inquiries, contributing to the depth of our understanding rather than serving as mere fodder for entertainment.

By dismantling these myths surrounding tachyons, we can elevate the discourse regarding superluminal particles and their theoretical foundations beyond the sensationalized boundaries typical of popular culture. As we endeavor to explore the implications of these particles through the lens of serious scientific inquiry, we emphasize a commitment to grounding discussions in empirical evidence and rigorous theory. Engaging with these complexities presents both challenges and opportunities for intellectual growth. A nuanced understanding of tachyons could hint at deeper truths about the universe, ever urging humanity to reconcile the known with the speculative. Through diligent inquiry, we may uncover new pathways to knowledge that reflect the multifaceted nature of existence itself.

3. The Scientific Pursuit: Historical Perspectives

3.1. Inception of Ideas: Ancient Philosophies on Speed

The ancient philosophies on speed, while rudimentary compared to today's intricate scientific frameworks, provide a fascinating backdrop for understanding the inception of ideas that ultimately contributed to the formation of tachyon theory. The perceptions of speed in various cultures and philosophical schools bear significant relevance to contemporary discourse on faster-than-light travel and superluminal particles such as tachyons. These early explorations and conceptions of motion and velocity not only influenced the evolution of physics but also set the stage for later dichotomies between physical science and metaphysical inquiry.

In antiquity, the relationship between speed and movement was deeply intertwined with notions of time and space. Philosophers, scientists, and mathematicians sought to comprehend the nature of reality through the lens of motion. The ancient Greeks, for example, presented a tapestry of ideas, where speed was often a subject of philosophical speculation. Pythagoras and his followers ventured into discussions surrounding the idea of harmony within motion, viewing speed as inherently linked to the way objects interact within the cosmos. Their insights suggested that speed could be perceived through a mathematical lens, leading to the foundational aspects of geometry that would characterize later scientific inquiries.

Aristotle contributed significantly to the philosophical debates on motion and speed, proposing that all objects possess a natural state of rest or uniform motion. His theories lacked the empirical analysis that modern physics employs, yet Aristotle's insistence that heavier objects fall faster illustrated a rudimentary understanding of acceleration—a precursor to the laws of motion articulated by Sir Isaac Newton centuries later. The dichotomy between natural motion and imposed motion sparked myriad conversations around the principles governing speed and how they interact with the flow of time.

During the Middle Ages, as ancient texts were rediscovered and philosophical thought flourished, scholars began to rekindle the discussions surrounding speed. The works of thinkers like Thomas Aquinas drew connections between spiritual realms and material existence, imbuing the concept of speed with metaphysical significance. This period saw the emergence of ideas that emphasized the interplay of time, motion, and divine purpose. The intricate discussions surrounding the divine speed of angels or celestial bodies would inspire later scientific inquiries into the nature of time and space.

The Islamic Golden Age further enriched philosophical discourse on motion and speed. Scholars like Al-Farabi and Ibn Sina (Avicenna) sought to reconcile Aristotelian concepts with emerging scientific practices. They presented sophisticated descriptions of motion while exploring ideas about renovation and eternity, framing their discussions within both empirical observations and theological contexts. The synthesis of observation and philosophy during this time would resonate through the ages, ultimately influencing the scientific revolution that lay ahead.

As we approached the dawn of the modern era, figures like Galileo Galilei made crucial contributions to the study of motion, laying the groundwork for classical mechanics. Galileo's experimental approach illuminated the importance of observation and measurement, helping to define the concept of speed as a quantifiable entity. His studies on pendulums, falling bodies, and uniform motion challenged preconceived notions and stripped down complex ideas into manageable concepts that would serve as a foundation for Newtonian physics. Moreover, his paradoxes regarding infinite divisibility and the nature of time foreshadowed the philosophical and scientific challenges encountered in subsequent discussions about tachyons and faster-than-light travel.

The enlightenment period and the rise of modern science brought forth further advancements in the understanding of speed, influenced significantly by developments in mathematics and physics. Isaac Newton's laws of motion employed rigorous mathematical frameworks that transformed the understanding of dynamics and speed. The integration of calculus allowed for differential analysis of motion, ushering in a new era where the pursuit of understanding speed became intertwined with the evolution of mathematical language. The implications of speed were now considered in the context of forces, masses, and energy—a trajectory leading towards sophisticated discussions about superluminal particles.

Pioneering thinkers of the 19th and early 20th centuries, including James Clerk Maxwell and Albert Einstein, radically reframed the understanding of speed and its relationship to light and time. Maxwell's equations brought forth the interconnectedness of electric and magnetic fields, suggesting that speed itself was not an isolated phenomenon but rather a component of a more extensive electromagnetic framework. Einstein's revolutionary theory of relativity further refined the notions of speed, presenting the idea that velocities near the speed of light produce profound effects on time—concepts that challenge anything one might have encountered during the early philosophical discussions surrounding speed.

By examining these ancient philosophies, we recognize the continuum through which ideas evolved. The inquiries into speed and motion laid not only the groundwork for classical mechanics but also opened dialogue for the speculative realms encountered in modern physics. The multifaceted approaches to understanding speed across cultures and epochs reveal a tapestry of intellectual engagements that transcend physics alone, inviting philosophical contemplation regarding time, existence, and the very structure of the universe.

As we transition towards the exploration of tachyons and their implications, the ancient philosophies on speed echo through time, serving as a reminder that the stories we spin around the nature of existence connect us across generations. Integrating the historical perspectives enables a holistic approach to understanding tachyons—not merely as abstract mathematical constructs but as an extension of humanity's relentless quest to comprehend the cosmos and our place within it. Through this lens, we can appreciate how ancient wisdom continues to inform and challenge our scientific inquiries into the superluminal particles of today, intertwining past concepts and future possibilities in the grand tapestry of knowledge.

3.2. The Pioneers: Key Figures in Particle Physics

The journey into the realm of particle physics and the theoretical constructs of tachyons inevitably leads us to the pioneers who laid the foundational groundwork for this inquiry. The trailblazers of this scientific field have not only shaped the discourse around subatomic particles but have also forged pathways leading toward the speculative notion of superluminal travel that tachyons represent. Their combined legacies are woven into the narrative of modern physics, each contributing unique ideas and insights that continue to inform contemporary understanding.

To appreciate the role of key figures in particle physics, we must consider the late 19th and early 20th centuries, an era marked by monumental shifts in scientific thought. One cannot start this discussion without mentioning Albert Einstein, a figure whose theoretical constructs revolutionized our grasp of time, space, and motion. While not directly involved in the original formulation of tachyons, Einstein's special theory of relativity laid the groundwork necessary for later explorations of faster-than-light phenomena. His radical assertion that the speed of light is the ultimate speed limit for massive particles presented a paradox that future physicists, including those theorizing about tachyons, would need to navigate. The imaginative leap required to propose that there could exist particles capable of moving faster than this established limit owes much to Einstein's challenging of conventional perceptions of speed and velocity.

Following in the footsteps of Einstein, we find Hermann Minkowski, whose exploration of four-dimensional spacetime crystallized concepts that would become pivotal in understanding tachyon dynamics.

His geometrical formulation of relativity transformed the interpretation of time and space as interwoven dimensions, rather than separate, linear pathways. Minkowski's ideas open the door to considering hypothetical particles like tachyons existing within a more expansive framework where traditional notions of velocity required reevaluation. His work, though not centered on tachyons per se, established a conceptual playground where subsequent theorists could explore the potential implications of superluminal particles.

The formal introduction of tachyons as a concept took flight under the pen of Gerald Feinberg in 1967. Feinberg notably coined the term "tachyon" to describe particles that theoretically possess imaginary mass, a departure from mass within the realm of conventional physics. His seminal paper argued for the existence of these superluminal particles, positing the consequences such entities would yield if they were to exist in the universe. Feinberg's pioneering theoretical framework was fundamental because it engaged critically with the implications of speed, energy, and causality. This connection demonstrated how tachyons could disrupt traditional views of spacetime and challenged physicists to grapple with the intricacies of particle behavior that went beyond established theories.

As the discussion around tachyons evolved, additional key figures emerged who contributed to the dialogue. For instance, Richard Feynman and his development of quantum electrodynamics provided a richer understanding of particle interactions, essential for situating tachyon theory within the broader tapestry of quantum mechanics. While Feynman's primary focus was not on superluminal particles, his work emphasized the complexities inherent in particle physics, which ultimately serves as a backdrop for speculative concepts like tachyons. His Feynman diagrams offered visual frameworks for understanding interactions at the quantum level, allowing future researchers to investigate potential ramifications of hypothetical particles within quantum field theory.

Martin Gardner, a prominent popularizer of science, played a crucial role in bringing concepts like tachyons into public consciousness through his writings. By engaging with both the scientific community and the layperson, Gardner not only demystified complex theories but also underscored the significance of speculative inquiries such as tachyons, calling attention to their profound philosophical implications. The importance of communicative figures like Gardner cannot be understated, as they cultivate public interest and facilitate discussions that bridge the gap between academia and everyday understanding.

As we delve deeper into contemporary contexts, the legacy of these pioneering minds persists. Current discussions on tachyons can be found interspersed with advancements in quantum field theory and cosmology, where advancements in experimental methods still explore the thresholds of particle behaviors which may suggest the presence of tachyonic phenomena. Furthermore, the new generation of physicists, inspired by the foundational work of figures like Feinberg and Feynman, is venturing into uncharted territories of theoretical physics to test the robustness of tachyon models against burgeoning empirical data.

In retrospect, the journey of tachyon research is a testament to the collective endeavors of these luminaries who have enriched our understanding of the universe. Their contributions form a rich tapestry that encapsulates not just the intricacies of superluminal particles but also the ongoing quest for knowledge and understanding of the cosmos. Through their innovative ideas, we are inspired to continue questioning the known, rethinking theoretical boundaries, and considering the speculative possibilities surrounding particles that may travel beyond the speed of light. As we look to the future of tachyon research, it is imperative to remember the footprints of those who paved the way, and the legacy they have gifted to generations yet to come. The story of tachyons is one intricately linked to the lives, thoughts, and imaginations of the pioneers in particle physics who dared to dream beyond the known limitations of our universe.

3.3. Breakthroughs and Discoveries

Significant breakthroughs and discoveries in the field of quantum mechanics have increasingly lent support to the speculative concept of tachyons, the elusive particles theorized to travel faster than light. As we probe deeper into the intricacies of the quantum realm, we encounter phenomena that resonate with the tachyonic narrative, inviting scientists and theorists alike to reconsider established principles of particle physics and the very fabric of reality.

One of the most important tenets of quantum mechanics is the behavior of particles at microscopic scales, where the classical laws of physics give way to a realm filled with uncertainty and probabilistic outcomes. Quantum mechanics reveals a universe in which particles can exist in multiple states simultaneously, characterized by the concept of superposition. This principle serves as a crucial foundation for understanding the implications of tachyons; if these particles exist, they would likely engage with quantum mechanics in ways that challenge our conventional treatment of speed and causality.

A pertinent example highlighting the parallel between quantum mechanics and tachyonic theory is the phenomenon of quantum tunneling. This effect, where particles can traverse energy barriers that they conventionally could not cross, raises intriguing questions about superluminal behavior. In quantum tunneling, it appears that particles can instantaneously appear on the other side of a barrier, suggesting a mechanism by which faster-than-light interactions might occur without violating the constraints set by relativity. This counters the intuitive understanding of motion as a linear progression, hinting at mechanisms in which tachyonic particles could play a role by allowing transitions across barriers that conventional physics does not accommodate, thus facilitating superluminal communication or travel.

Moreover, the enigmatic realm of quantum entanglement presents another fascinating avenue of exploration as we investigate tachyon dynamics. In this phenomenon, two or more particles become correlated in such a way that the state of one instantly impacts the state of the other, regardless of the distance separating them. This apparent "instantaneous" connection challenges the classical notions of locality and causality, compelling us to reassess our understanding of the relationships that underlie the universe. If tachyons exist, their potential ability to facilitate faster-than-light communication may provide insight into the mysterious connections observable in entangled particles. The exploration of tachyonic mechanisms could deepen our comprehension of how matter communicates and interacts across vast distances, moving us closer to bridging the gaps in information transfer that remain so perplexing in contemporary physics.

Additionally, examination of quantum field theories has opened the door to considering tachyons within a more formalized mathematical structure. Many theoretical physicists entertain models that incorporate tachyons into the framework of quantum field theory, exploring the implications of superluminal particles and how they might interact with our known particles and fields. Such models may suggest alterations to the existing understanding of mass, energy interactions, and field dynamics—paving the way for potential breakthroughs in how we perceive the relationship between different particles in the universe.

Empirical investigations have also begun to probe into the intersection of tachyons and established particles. Researchers have sought observable phenomena that may provide indications of tachyonic behavior or interactions, though direct evidence remains elusive. Nevertheless, advanced experiments, particularly at high-energy particle colliders, attempt to detect signatures or patterns in particle interactions that could hint at tachyon-like characteristics. Such experimental pursuits are crucial as they may unearth insights that reshape our understanding of particle interactions while bolstering or refuting the concept of tachyons.

As breakthroughs in quantum mechanics continue to unfold, the scientific community is increasingly compelled to engage in discussions that encompass both theoretical and experimental dimensions of tachyon research. These pivotal discoveries encourage us to challenge classical paradigms regarding reality, speed, and causality, urging us to explore the implications of a universe that may harbor faster-than-light phenomena. The intersections of quantum mechanics and tachyonic theory illuminate a pathway fundamentally reshaping our comprehension of existence, promising to unveil mysteries that have captivated the minds of physicists and philosophers alike for generations.

In conclusion, significant breakthroughs in quantum mechanics not only lend support to the existence of tachyons but also highlight the pressing need for a robust scientific inquiry into superluminal particles. The ongoing dialogues within the scientific community serve as a reminder of the complex interplay between theoretical speculation and empirical evidence, pushing us to consider new frontiers of exploration in our quest to understand the nature of our universe. As we venture forward, the realm of tachyons stands as a tantalizing frontier, embodying both the complexities of modern physics and the limitless possibilities that lie beyond the speed of light.

3.4. Tachyons in the Modern Scientific Discourse

In the contemporary scientific discourse, tachyons emerge as a subject of fascination and contention among physicists, providing a valuable lens through which we can explore the boundaries of modern physics and the unresolved mysteries of the universe. These hypothetical particles, theorized to exceed the speed of light, challenge conventional wisdom founded on Einstein's relativity, prompting ongoing investigations into their implications on energy, causality, and the very nature of spacetime.

The historical context of tachyon research reveals how the inception of these ideas is not a sudden phenomenon; rather, it is interwoven with the threads of significant scientific advancements. The gradual evolution of concepts surrounding speed, time, and the fundamental structure of reality laid the groundwork for considering superluminal particles. As early as the 20th century, thinkers like Hermann Minkowski and Gerald Feinberg began to shift perspectives on how particles might behave under conditions that defy standard physical laws. Their work marked the intersection of abstract theory with practical inquiry, setting the stage for a dialogue that continues to evolve within modern physics.

In the present day, tachyons are increasingly discussed in the context of various theoretical frameworks, including quantum mechanics and cosmology. As researchers endeavor to reconcile grim realities in astrophysics—such as dark matter and dark energy—with proposed models incorporating tachyons, the scientific community witnesses a reinvigoration of debate around phenomena that defy classical interpretations. The speculative nature of tachyons invites a collaborative spirit among physicists, cosmologists, and philosophers alike, promoting an interdisciplinary exploration whereby insights from one field might illuminate discoveries in another.

Central to the discussion of tachyons is the question of causality—a principle that undergirds our understanding of physical law. The potential violation of causality through the existence of tachyons leads to paradoxes that stimulate rich philosophical inquiries regarding time and existence. Furthermore, tachyon-mediated communication has inspired imaginative proposals for breakthroughs in technology that transcend existing communication speeds. Yet, these discussions remain tethered to rigorous examination, demanding evidence that can bridge the gap between speculation and established science.

As we interrogate the modern scientific discourse surrounding tachyons, it becomes apparent that their relevance is sustained not only by theoretical curiosity but also by empirical pursuits aimed at uncovering potential experimental signatures. Various avenues of exploration—ranging from high-energy particle collision experiments to astrophysical observations—provide a canvas for probing tachyon theories in the laboratory and beyond. The interplay of theory and experiment fosters a continuous dialogue where confirmation of tachyon models would mark a paradigm shift in our understanding of the universe.

Bear in mind that the dialogue surrounding tachyons is not without its obstacles. Many scientists express skepticism rooted in concerns regarding the fundamental implications of superluminal particles on foundational physical principles. These criticisms often spark fruitful conversations, propelling researchers to rigorously evaluate their hypotheses and refine their conceptual frameworks. In recognizing the skepticism within the scientific community, we underscore its role in catalyzing deeper understanding and fostering robust inquiry.

Overall, the concept of tachyons serves as a challenging and provocative frontier in modern science. Emerging from a rich tapestry of historical ideas, contemporary inquiries reaffirm the importance of vigilant investigation and imaginative speculation. As physicists strive to navigate the complexities of the universe, tachyons symbolize both the limits of our current understanding and the tantalizing potential that lies just beyond—inviting us to ponder the extraordinary realms of existence, speed, and the eventual unraveling of cosmic mysteries.

3.5. Obstacles and Criticisms Over the Decades

Throughout the decades, the discourse surrounding tachyons has faced considerable obstacles and criticisms, reflecting both the complexities inherent in theoretical physics and the challenges of reconciling speculative ideas with established scientific principles. As scientists and theorists have attempted to probe the implications and potential existence of tachyons—hypothetical particles that purportedly travel faster than light—their efforts have met with skepticism, ranging from methodological challenges to philosophical dilemmas.

One of the foremost obstacles in the pursuit of tachyon research is grounded in the very framework of Einstein's theory of relativity, which posits that nothing can surpass the speed of light without violating fundamental laws of physics. This widely accepted principle has long constituted a cornerstone of modern physics. Consequently, the idea that particles could exist with the capacity for superluminal motion challenges core assumptions regarding mass, energy, and causality. The theoretical underpinning of tachyons, which suggests they possess an imaginary mass, leads critics to assert that such a notion defies physical reality and remains disconnected from empirical validation.

In the realm of experimental physics, scientific inquiry into tachyonic particles faces formidable hurdles as well. The identification or production of tachyons has not been achieved in laboratory settings despite years of investigation. Many researchers have sought specific signatures or interactions that might indicate the presence of tachyonic behavior, but the lack of concrete empirical evidence has fueled skepticism about their existence. Attempts to design experiments that could compellingly support tachyon theories often encounter intricate technical limitations and the inherent unpredictability of particle interactions at high energies. This situation propels debates about the feasibility of discovering tachyons using current methodologies and leads many to question whether the concept itself is scientifically valid or if it resides primarily within the realm of speculative physics.

Moreover, critics contend that the theories surrounding tachyons can lead to paradoxes and contradictions that undermine their scientific integrity. The hypothetical implications of tachyonic behavior, particularly regarding causality, present philosophical conundrums that reflect the complexity of time and motion. If tachyons were to exist, it raises the question of whether effects could precede causes, thus challenging our linear and intuitive understanding of time's arrow. This discussion often emerges in philosophical forums, creating a fundamental divide between those who seek to reconcile tachyon theories with existing frameworks and those who regard them as untenable. The tension between philosophical inquiry and scientific rigor frequently complicates discussions about the validity of tachyon research, further polarizing opinions within the community.

As discussions around tachyons proliferated, they also faced critiques of being intertwined with pseudoscience or speculative fiction. Some skeptics argue that the theoretical pursuits in tachyon research often resemble storytelling more than empirical science. This skepticism is compounded when popular media depicts tachyons in sensational forms, amplifying misunderstandings about scientific principles while simultaneously inviting the public to engage with dauntingly complex ideas through an entertaining lens. Critics often caution that conflating science with entertainment diminishes the rigor essential to proper scientific discourse, thus creating a broader reluctance to take tachyon research seriously among some circles of the scientific community.

Additionally, funding constraints pose significant challenges to tachyon research. As scientific funding becomes increasingly competitive, prioritization often favors established fields with clearer applications and demonstrable outcomes. Theoretical exploration of tachyons frequently occupies a niche space in physics that might not resonate with immediate practical benefits, leading to the marginalization of research efforts. This dynamic emphasizes the precarious balancing act that scientists must navigate between pushing the boundaries of theoretical inquiry and securing the necessary resources to support their work. The inability to connect the investigation of tachyons to tangible technological advancements further compounds the struggle to gain traction within the scientific community.

In working to overcome these obstacles, proponents of tachyonic theories often emphasize the interdisciplinary nature of the inquiry surrounding superluminal particles. By drawing connections between tachyon research and established principles within quantum mechanics, cosmology, and theoretical physics, advocates aim to integrate the study of tachyons within broader scientific narratives. This effort underscores the importance of an open dialogue that embraces both skepticism and curiosity—acknowledging the complexity of the questions at stake while advocating for an exploration of ideas that expand our understanding of the universe.

Thus, the decades-long journey of tachyon research embodies a rich tapestry of challenges and criticisms that reflect the broader struggles within the scientific process. From grappling with deeply ingrained paradigms to addressing empirical uncertainty and philosophical dilemmas, scientists engaged in this field are tasked with pushing the frontiers of knowledge while contending with skepticism and criticism at multiple levels. As they strive to envision a reality where superluminal particles may hold sway over the laws of nature, it is imperative to balance innovative theoretical pursuits with the methodological rigor that sustains the scientific enterprise—a journey marred by obstacles yet brimming with the promise of discovery. The ongoing discourse around tachyons compels us to engage critically with the intersections of theory, experimentation, and philosophical contemplation as we navigate the complexities defining our efforts to understand existence itself.

4. Quantum Mechanics and Tachyons

4.1. Quantum Theory Basics: The Fabric of Reality

In the realm of modern physics, quantum mechanics serves as a foundational pillar that reshapes our understanding of the universe. This field of study introduces complex and often counterintuitive principles governing the behavior of particles at a subatomic level. Within this framework, tachyons—hypothetical particles theorized to move faster than light—emerge as fascinating constructs that challenge traditional notions of speed, time, and the very fabric of reality. To grasp the significance of tachyons, we must first navigate the principles of quantum mechanics that underpin their theoretical existence.

Quantum mechanics operates on principles that diverge fundamentally from classical physics. At its core lies the concept of quantization, which posits that energy, momentum, and other physical quantities can only exist in discrete amounts or "quanta." This discrete nature challenges classical notions of continuous interaction and opens the door to phenomena that resist straightforward explanations. For instance, particles are no longer viewed merely as localized entities; rather, they exhibit wave-like characteristics, existing in states of superposition until observed or measured. This wave-particle duality introduces a profound depth to how we comprehend the nature of existence.

As we delve further into the implications of quantum theory, it becomes clear that achieving a coherent understanding of tachyons necessitates an exploration of their relationship with the principles underpinning quantum mechanics. Tachyons are theorized to travel at superluminal speeds and possess imaginary mass, thereby defying conventional physics that forbids any particle with real mass from reaching or exceeding the speed of light. This characteristic alone situates tachyons in a unique conceptual space where time and causality are redefined, prompting theoretical physicists to reconceptualize their models of particle behavior.

Understanding tachyons through the prism of quantum mechanics invites us to consider frameworks such as quantum field theory (QFT), which describes particles as excitations in underlying fields permeating the universe. In this paradigm, interactions are not isolated events but are part of a larger tapestry where entities exist simultaneously in multiple states. If tachyons were to exist, they could be perceived as excitations that traverse dimensions beyond our conventional understanding, furthering our exploration of causality and communication methods.

Wave-particle duality plays a significant role in the proposed framework for tachyons. In this duality, particles like electrons can behave as both particles and waves, embracing the probabilities defining their traits. This suggests that tachyons, if they exist, could also embody this duality, raising intriguing questions about how superluminal particles interact with slower-moving entities. Their wave nature may allow them to engage in phenomena resembling quantum tunneling, where particles can "bypass" barriers. What if tachyons could bypass temporal barriers as well, opening channels for communication across vast distances instantaneously?

The implications of quantum superposition—a state in which a particle exists in multiple configurations simultaneously—serve as an exciting premise for contemplating the behavior of tachyons within quantum systems. This duality prompts us to envision scenarios where tachyons could facilitate instantaneous interactions between particles across great distances, challenging our understanding of locality and communication. In this realm, tachyons introduce additional dimensions of interplay between quantum states, potentially reshaping perspectives on unobserved influences on time and causality.

Moreover, entangled particles provide a compelling context within quantum mechanics that parallels the proposed behavior of tachyons. Quantum entanglement establishes connections between particles irrespective of the space that separates them. When one particle in an entangled pair is manipulated, the other instantaneously changes, regardless of the physical distance—an effect that some interpret as a form of superluminal communication. The exploration of tachyons prompts us to consider whether these faster-than-light particles could operate in a similar vein, allowing for instantaneous interactions and connections that defy classical interpretations of space and time.

In the broader landscape of quantum mechanics, the mathematical frameworks employed to understand particle behavior also underscore the potential existence of tachyons. Quantum field equations can accommodate solutions suggesting superluminal behavior, prompting physicists to investigate models that allow for the emergence of tachyons within the established probabilistic landscape of quantum mechanics. Such investigations harmonize with ongoing efforts to bridge the gap between theoretical constructs and empirical validation, fostering a dialogue that emphasizes the importance of rigorous experimentation and robust reasoning.

As we explore tachyons' intersection with quantum mechanics, we recognize that these hypothetical particles represent an invitation to rethink our understanding of existence. Through engaging with the principles of quantum theory, we unveil a rich tapestry of ideas that challenge conventional perceptions of reality, causality, and speed. The pursuit of tachyons may illuminate pathways for future research that transcends established paradigms, enriching our comprehension of the cosmic mysteries woven intricately into the fabric of the universe. This journey through quantum mechanics and its implications for tachyons beckons us to ponder profound questions about the nature of time, space, and humanity's quest for knowledge in an ever-expanding cosmos.

4.2. Wave-Particle Duality and Tachyons

The duality of wave and particle characteristics is a fundamental principle embedded in the core of quantum mechanics. It challenges our classical understanding of the physical world, where entities are typically classified strictly as either waves or particles. Instead, quantum mechanics presents a more complex interplay, wherein particles can exhibit properties of both, depending on how they are observed or measured. This concept becomes particularly compelling when we consider the hypothetical nature of tachyons, particles theorized to traverse faster than light. In exploring how tachyons might fit within this wave-particle duality paradigm, we are compelled to investigate the implications of such a framework on our understanding of existence, communication, and even time itself.

At the heart of wave-particle duality lies the notion that particles like electrons and photons do not adhere neatly to one category. Rather, they exist in a superposition of states, represented mathematically by wave functions. These wave functions describe probabilities: the likelihood of finding a particle in a particular position or state when measured. When an observation occurs, the wave function collapses into a definite state, resulting in what we perceive as manifestations of either particle or wave behavior. This phenomenon leads us to question the very nature of tachyons, and whether they too can be encapsulated within the wave-particle framework.

If tachyons exist, their ability to exceed the speed of light suggests that they would inherently operate within this dual nature. Theoretical frameworks propose that tachyons could be represented by wave functions that encapsulate both superluminal motion and the oscillatory properties of waves. Within this representation, tachyons would not be restricted solely to conventional trajectories, but could instead exist in a space that combines characteristics of both wave-like interference patterns and particle-like impacts. This could fundamentally redefine our understanding of how entities communicate and interact across time and space.

Considering the wave aspect of tachyons, one might imagine scenarios in which their faster-than-light nature facilitates unique wave patterns that resonate across vast distances, transcending traditional limitations of speed communication. In such cases, tachyons could potentially transmit information or signals instantaneously through their wave-like properties, enabling connections that evade the constraints imposed by relativity. This leads us to envision applications in future technologies that harness these characteristics to develop unprecedented methods of communication, perhaps allowing instantaneous transfer of information regardless of spatial separation.

Moreover, the interplay between tachyons and the observer effect —a principle wherein the act of observation influences the state of a quantum system—introduces profound implications for the nature of reality. If tachyons exist and are indeed detectable, their wave functions may collapse upon observation into superluminal states, prompting questions about the broader implications such collapses might have on our understanding of causality. The traditional notion of cause-and-effect relationships reliant upon linear timelines could be upended if tachyons are part of a continuum where effects can precede their causes.

Another intriguing aspect to consider is the relationship between tachyon dynamics and phenomena such as quantum tunneling. In quantum mechanics, particles have been observed to "tunnel" through barriers they seemingly should not be able to cross, suggesting non-classical pathways of interaction. If tachyons exist as superluminal particles, they could potentially undergo tunneling behaviors that defy spatial confines, allowing them to bridge temporal barriers similarly. Thus, it stands to reason that the behaviors of tachyons could not only serve as a scientific investigation into the nature of immediate interactions but also pose philosophical inquiries regarding the fabric of reality.

Yet, while exploring the potential of tachyons within the wave-particle duality framework offers exciting avenues of thought, it is imperative that we balance speculation with rigorous scientific inquiry. The existence of tachyons remains unproven, and the implications they carry challenge widely accepted frameworks of particle physics, incorporating ideas that oscillate between established science and speculative theory. As we delve into the exploration of tachyons through the lens of wave-particle duality, we must be grounded in empirical scrutiny while remaining open to the profound ideas that challenge our conventional worldviews.

Ultimately, understanding tachyons within the wave-particle duality invites us to reimagine possibilities within the quantum realm and beyond. This speculative journey affords us the opportunity to delve into questions that transcend our traditional comprehendible universe, exploring realms wherein time, causality, and communication dance in a complexity yet to be fully deciphered. As we continue to navigate the intricacies of tachyon theory and its potential implications, we embrace the challenge of balancing scientific inquiry with the imaginative exploration of ideas that may one day reshape our understanding of the universe.

4.3. Quantum Tunneling: A Precedent for Superluminal Particles

Quantum tunneling represents one of the most intriguing phenomena in quantum mechanics, allowing particles to transition through energy barriers that, according to classical physics, they should not be able to traverse. This seemingly magical ability has prompted scientists to explore its implications across various fields, including the speculative domain of faster-than-light particles such as tachyons. By examining the principles of quantum tunneling, we glean insights that resonate with the possibilities and challenges surrounding tachyon dynamics, suggesting that there may already exist precedents in quantum physics hinting at the potential for superluminal behavior.

At its core, quantum tunneling arises from the wave nature of particles. In classical frameworks, a particle's energy is strictly confined to specific thresholds, rendering it impossible to cross barriers that exceed those energy levels. However, in quantum mechanics, particles are represented by wave functions that describe probabilities across varying states. When particles encounter a barrier, the probability wave can extend into and even beyond it, allowing for a non-zero chance that the particle will appear on the other side, despite not having the requisite energy to cross in the classical sense. This concept fundamentally challenges the classical notion of linear motion, instead portraying particles as existing in probabilistic states.

This remarkable behavior of quantum tunneling underscores the flexibility within quantum mechanics, where the definitions of motion, interaction, and causality can differ drastically from classical intuitions. Further exploration of this phenomenon reveals that, under certain conditions, tunneling can appear to occur instantaneously. While these interactions do not imply superluminal travel in the traditional sense, they lay a conceptual foundation suggesting that particles can behave in ways that defy classical limitations.

Now, as we extend this framework to encompass tachyons, the discussion evolves into one of possibility rather than mere speculation. Tachyons, hypothesized to possess imaginary mass, would theoretically inhabit a state where they could continuously move faster than light. Their existence would capitalize on the behavior of energy and spacetime in ways that challenge established interpretations of causality. If we accept that particles can exhibit behavior like tunneling, where boundaries can be circumvented, it stands to reason that tachyons could similarly traverse barriers of velocity that define our current understanding of motion—speed limits that are capped at light speed for massive particles.

Additionally, the quantum tunneling effect highlights the non-locality characteristic of quantum mechanics, where actions performed at one location can instantaneously affect states at another, a concept that echoes in discussions around entangled particles. These connections invite analogies with the potential for tachyon communication or influences that occur instantaneously, despite spatial separation. The understanding that particles can "leak" through barriers suggests an avenue wherein tachyons might influence neighboring systems without the need for conventional interactions defined by light speed limitations.

Moreover, some researchers propose that observing quantum tunneling might yield indirect evidence supporting the existence of tachyons or similar phenomena. For instance, if tunneling events were to manifest under specific conditions that align closely with theoretical tachyon behaviors, they could provide observational insights into superluminal interactions. Such observations would not only bolster the theoretical frameworks but could inspire new experimental designs aimed at isolating and understanding these enigmatic particles.

As we ponder the implications of quantum tunneling for the existence of tachyons, we recognize that exploring these interrelated phenomena propels us into a frontier filled with rich inquiries about the nature of reality, speed, and the vast complexities of the universe. The intersection of these discussions invokes profound questions, compelling scientists to examine not only the behaviors seen in quantum physics but the broader implications these behaviors hold for understanding time, communication, and the potential for technologies that operate outside of our current grasp.

In summary, quantum tunneling provides a compelling precedent for considering tachyons as more than theoretical constructs; it introduces a narrative wherein faster-than-light behavior is not merely an abstract idea but rooted in the principles that govern the quantum world. As we continue to explore these connections, we may uncover pathways that not only deepen our understanding of tachyons but also expand the horizons of theoretical physics, prompting us to rethink the very fabric of existence itself. The echoes of quantum tunneling signal possible avenues where the boundaries of science blur into realms long relegated to speculation, inviting a renewed exploration of our universe's mysterious and perhaps unfathomable depths.

4.4. Entanglement and Tachyons

Entanglement presents a strikingly fascinating aspect of quantum mechanics, exemplifying a net of interconnectedness among particles that challenges intuitive perceptions of separateness and locality. Within the context of superluminal particles like tachyons, understanding entanglement becomes pivotal not just for comprehending their potential properties but also for addressing the implications they could carry for communication, causality, and the fundamental fabric of the universe.

Quantum entanglement arises when two or more particles become so intricately linked that their individual states can no longer be described independently. Instead, the state of one particle instantly correlates with the state of another, regardless of the distance separating them. This instantaneous influence, which Einstein famously critiqued as "spooky action at a distance," suggests a connection that defies classical spatial constraints. The implications of this phenomenon reach far, igniting inquiries into the very nature of reality and the mechanics of communication across vast expanses of space.

The theoretical existence of tachyons—hypothetical particles that can travel faster than light—introduces an intriguing dimension to the discourse surrounding entanglement. If tachyons exert any influence on entangled particles, their dynamics could operate under mechanisms that transcend the conventional boundaries of cause and effect. Theoretically, if these faster-than-light particles are real, the interaction between entangled pairs might include tachyonic influences that facilitate instantaneous communication or correlations that operate independently of light-speed limitations.

One can imagine a scenario where the instantaneous change in state of an entangled particle could be mediated by a tachyon. This potential exists within the framework of quantum field theories that incorporate tachyon dynamics more formally. While entanglement traditionally operates under the premise that information transfer cannot exceed light speed, the incorporation of tachyons posits a radical restructuring of this understanding. In such a model, the presence of a tachyon could act as an intermediary, linking entangled particles in ways that allow faster-than-light communication—or at least, influencing observations in ways still consistent with relativistic principles.

Furthermore, the characteristic of entangled particles, which can exhibit correlations even when separated by vast distances, raises intriguing questions about how tachyons might influence these interactions. If tachyons do exist, one could theorize that their potential to traverse dimensions beyond the constraints of spacetime could create novel pathways for influencing the behavior of entangled particles. Perhaps tachyons could transport information or correlations instantaneously, circumventing the conventional delay imposed within the speed-of-light framework.

However, the relationship between tachyons and entanglement also prompts critical scrutiny of fundamental principles governing modern physics. The interference of tachyonic influences might challenge conventional understandings of causality, prompting a reevaluation of cause-effect relationships. If influences can propagate instantaneously through tachyons, it raises inquiries about the linearity of time and whether specific outcomes can precede their initiating causes. Such a scenario beckons the possibility of temporal paradoxes typically associated with time travel, complicating our current models of how particles and events relate across temporal dimensions.

Delving deeper into the mathematical frameworks of quantum mechanics, we find that concepts like the Born rule—used to calculate probabilities of outcomes in quantum systems—could adapt to incorporate tachyonic interactions, establishing new probabilities that align with superluminal dynamics. Researchers may explore scenarios where existing models could be expanded to account for these hypothetical particles, leading to a more comprehensive understanding of both entangled behaviors and tachyonic influences.

In light of this discussion, it becomes evident that the synthesis of entanglement and tachyon theories represents a rich intellectual frontier. By interrogating the intersections between these phenomena, researchers embark on a journey toward unveiling deeper truths within the quantum domain, enhancing our comprehension of speed, locality, and the very nature of reality.

While methodological and experimental challenges remain in defining and detecting tachyons, the conceptual dialogue they inspire reflects humanity's enduring curiosity about the cosmos. The interplay between entanglement and tachyons ignites speculative imaginations, prompting investigations into the profound questions surrounding existence and the mysterious threads that connect every particle in our universe.

In conclusion, exploring entanglement through the lens of superluminal particles like tachyons holds transformative potential for both theoretical inquiry and our understanding of the universe. By marrying these concepts, we form a framework where reality becomes a tapestry of interwoven influences—where distance may blur, causality is redefined, and knowledge beckons from realms yet undiscovered. The dialogue surrounding entanglement and tachyons invites a reimagining of the underlying assumptions about interaction, time, and the very nature of the universe we inhabit, bridging speculative science with philosophical inquiry in ways that stretch the imagination.

4.5. Quantum Field Theory: Incorporating Tachyons

The incorporation of tachyons into the fabric of quantum field theory represents a bold and potentially revolutionary undertaking in theoretical physics, bridging the realms of established particle physics with speculative propositions. Quantum field theory itself operates at the intersection of quantum mechanics and special relativity, allowing us to view particles not as isolated entities but as excitations in underlying fields. By proposing tachyons—hypothetical particles that travel faster than light—into this framework, scientists are tasked with reconsidering fundamental principles governing energy, causality, and the very nature of spacetime.

Surrounding the discussion of tachyons are intricate mathematical structures that allow theoretical physicists to articulate their properties. One crucial element is the distinction between massive and massless particles, with tachyons categorized as particles possessing "imaginary mass." This theoretical attribute results in unique energy-momentum relationships that diverge from those of observable particles. In a conventional setup, the energy of a particle is described by the equation $E^2 = p^2c^2 + m^2c^4$. For tachyons, derivatives of this equation imply that as their energy decreases, their velocity increases, presenting an intriguing contradiction to the classical picture of particle dynamics.

Expanding upon the mathematical foundation of quantum field theory, researchers have utilized Lagrangian formulations to explore interactions involving tachyons. These formulations provide a systematic way of deriving equations of motion for various fields while integrating potential tachyonic contributions. By incorporating tachyonic fields into existing models, scientists can theorize potential behaviors and interactions while scrutinizing how these superluminal particles might impact established theories like the Standard Model of particle physics.

One theoretical backdrop for tachyons comes from the exploration of spontaneous symmetry breaking within quantum field theories. Certain frameworks propose that if tachyons exist, they might influence fields in such a way that would lead to mass generation through non-standard mechanisms. This addresses the question of how vacuum expectations could couple with tachyonic particles, influencing the properties of other field excitations while opening doors to new interactions previously unconsidered.

The implications of tachyons are not solely restricted to abstract theoretical considerations; they extend into potential applications across various fields. For instance, the realm of quantum communication might reap significant benefits from the existence of tachyons. Hypothetical constructs suggest that if tachyons could be harnessed, they might facilitate instantaneous transmission of information or influence across vast distances, effectively redefining communication paradigms. This tantalizing prospect invites rigorous inquiry into how tachyon signals might materially translate into technological advancements.

However, the notion of incorporating tachyons brings forth deeper philosophical investigations. The successful integration of tachyons into quantum field theory warrants an exploration into the ramifications for causality—one of the bedrock principles underpinning our understanding of the universe. Causality is intrinsically linked to time's arrow, and the potential for tachyonic interference could suggest a world where effects might precede causes, challenging our conventional timelines.

The quest for empirical evidence to substantiate the existence of tachyons also assumes a significant role in the discourse surrounding quantum field theories. Current experimental endeavors strive to test the limits of these theories, with scientists seeking to identify signatures reminiscent of tachyonic interactions. By examining high-energy collisions and phenomena within cosmic rays, researchers hope to unveil quantifiable evidence that could either affirm or challenge the theoretical frameworks wherein tachyons dwell.

In closing, the incorporation of tachyons into quantum field theory represents not merely an extension of particle physics but invites rich dialogue across multiple dimensions of scientific inquiry and philosophical thought. Navigating this landscape requires a delicate balance of theoretical rigor and speculative imagination as we endeavor to grasp the potential implications of superluminal particles. As researchers continue their quests to explore this expansive frontier, tachyons may very well redefine our interpretations of speed, time, and the universe itself, standing at the threshold of a new era in scientific understanding.

5. Cosmology: Tachyons in the Universe

5.1. The Expanding Universe Theory

The accelerating expansion of the universe, a phenomenon extensively documented and analyzed by astronomers and cosmologists, sparks significant intrigue regarding the fundamental mechanics underlying this cosmic evolution. While traditional understandings involve a confluence of dark energy and matter, an increasingly fascinating intersection emerges when considering how tachyons—hypothetical particles projected to travel faster than light—might relate to this expansive motion of the cosmos. Exploring this connection not only delves into the nature of tachyons themselves but also sheds light on potential implications for our grasp on time, space, and the universe's very structure.

The concept of an expanding universe is grounded in observations that galaxies are receding from us at high velocities, a reality established by Edwin Hubble's landmark discovery of the redshift—an effect attributed to the Doppler effect on light emitted from these galaxies. Such observations suggest that the universe is not static; rather, it is in a continual state of dynamic flux, stretching and evolving over time. Dark energy has emerged as a proposed explanation for this acceleration—a mysterious force counteracting gravitational pull, leading to the observed increase in the rate of expansion. However, alongside this conventional framework, tachyons introduce riveting possibilities, potentially redefining our understanding of cosmic acceleration.

If tachyons exist and can influence cosmic dynamics, they might serve as agents driving the acceleration of the universe. Within theoretical frameworks, the idea that these particles could interact with existing forms of energy—dark energy, for instance—opens doors to fresh interpretations regarding how energy manifests throughout the cosmos. Since tachyons are theorized to possess imaginary mass and an ability to lose energy while gaining speed, their populous existence could generate effects that ripple through spacetime, perhaps contributing to the repulsive forces attributed to dark energy.

Moreover, if tachyons enable faster-than-light interactions, they could provide theoretical pathways for communication or transfer of energy across vast distances. In essence, cosmic phenomena—including the behavior and distribution of galaxies—might respond to influences from tachyonic particles that facilitate instantaneous, or superluminal, connections within the framework of the universe. This interplay between tachyons and cosmic evolution fosters discussions around whether they serve as mediators of energy that may trace back to the very origins of the universe itself.

In our quest to understand how tachyons might relate to the expansion of the universe, one must also confront the philosophical and scientific implications of permitting faster-than-light phenomena within our cosmological models. The introduction of tachyons necessitates a reevaluation of established principles that govern the laws of physics, particularly concerning causality. The relationship between tachyons and cosmic acceleration could lead to revolutionary ideas regarding the very nature of time—fueling inquiries about how temporal mechanics would interact with superluminal particles that traverse epochs within the universe.

Furthermore, if tachyons are woven into the fabric of astrophysical phenomena, they could take a central role in cosmological models aimed at unraveling the mysteries of dark matter and dark energy. Given that these enigmatic components constitute the majority of the universe's total energy density yet remain poorly understood, establishing a potential link between tachyon dynamics and these forces invites speculative inquiries about the universe's composition. The hypothetical properties of tachyons—while remaining theoretical —may guide scientists toward deeper explorations into the unseen frameworks that govern cosmic behavior.

In conclusion, the synthesis of tachyon theory with the expanding universe presents a narrative rich with potential and intrigue. By probing the implications of tachyons as potentially influencing the universe's acceleration, we open doors to novel approaches in cosmology, prompting profound inquiries about the nature of speed, time, and existence itself. Such explorations will teach us not only about the mechanics of the cosmos but also about our broader aspirations to understand the universe's most profound secrets—testing the limits of our knowledge in the radiant quest to traverse the vastness of existence.

5.2. Dark Matter and Dark Energy: The Tachyon Connection

The exploration of dark matter and dark energy has emerged as a leading frontier in modern cosmology, inviting scientists to delve into the uncharted territories of the universe that remain obscured from our observational capabilities. As we grapple with the enigmatic properties and behaviors of these cosmic components, an intriguing hypothesis arises: could tachyons, the hypothetical particles theorized to travel faster than light, serve as a crucial link in unraveling the mysteries of dark matter and dark energy?

Dark matter, as currently understood, is believed to comprise approximately 27% of the universe's total mass-energy content. Despite its significant contribution, it has proven elusive to direct detection, remaining invisible to the electromagnetic spectrum—making it undetectable through traditional means. The gravitational effects of dark matter can be observed indirectly, evidenced by phenomena such as galaxy rotation curves and gravitational lensing, which suggest that significant amounts of mass exist in regions where we see none. The challenge lies in identifying the fundamental constituents of dark matter, as various candidates—including Weakly Interacting Massive Particles (WIMPs), axions, and sterile neutrinos—have been proposed, yet none have been confirmed.

In this context, the theoretical underpinnings of tachyons offer a fresh perspective. Tachyons are posited to possess imaginary mass, meaning their properties diverge radically from those of known particles carrying positive mass. This unique combination of characteristics could explain aspects of dark matter that lend themselves to superluminal behavior. For instance, if tachyons can interact with matter in unconventional ways, they may contribute to gravitational effects observable in galactic structures without presenting the detectable signatures associated with conventional particles. By looking at dark matter through the lens of tachyon dynamics, we uncover a path that integrates higher-dimensional physics into our understanding, challenging traditional paradigms about mass, forces, and interactions.

Similarly, the concept of dark energy, which constitutes nearly 68% of the universe's total mass-energy content, poses another enigma. This mysterious force accelerates the expansion of the universe, leading to the phenomenon known as cosmic inflation. The exact nature of dark energy remains one of cosmology's most profound questions, with potential explanations ranging from cosmological constants to dynamic field theories. The connection with tachyons becomes particularly compelling when we consider the mechanism by which tachyons, if they exist, interact across spacetime. Their superluminal motion introduces the possibility of repulsive interactions, uniquely situating them as potential mediators of the forces attributed to dark energy.

The acceleration of the universe's expansion invites concepts rooted in the dynamics of tachyon fields. If tachyons pervade the cosmic landscape, their influence may manifest as a subtle yet profound impact on cosmic acceleration, facilitating interactions that defy classical interpretations of gravity and expansion. Integrating tachyon models into our understanding of dark energy could provide a framework in which the enigmatic properties of this force become more comprehensible, ultimately leading to new methodologies for empirical investigations.

Investigating the role of tachyons in explaining dark matter and dark energy necessitates a re-examination of current astrophysical models and their relationships with experimental physics. Proposed theoretical frameworks could assist researchers in evaluating intricate interactions between tachyonic particles and other cosmic constituents, thereby shedding light on the elusive dark components of our universe. These exploratory inquiries might yield novel predictions that could be tested through sophisticated observational techniques or high-energy experiments, helping to bridge the gap between theory and empirical validation.

Moreover, the interplay between tachyon dynamics and the fundamental structure of spacetime emerges as a critical avenue of exploration. The existence of tachyons could indicate an underlying framework where faster-than-light behavior fundamentally reshapes our understanding of the universe, disrupting existing paradigms and inspiring the formulation of new theories. A deeper examination of tachyons may ignite a paradigm shift in how we articulate the relationships among gravity, energy, and the actual fabric of reality itself.

In essence, synthesizing the concepts of tachyons with the mysteries of dark matter and dark energy beckons a reconfiguration of our cosmological narrative, enriching our comprehension of the cosmos. Imagining a universe intertwined with superluminal particles nudges us toward philosophical inquiries surrounding the nature of existence, pushing the boundaries of our scientific understanding. As researchers begin to explore the potential connections between tachyons and the elusive forces of dark matter and dark energy, we stand at the precipice of a new frontier in understanding the universe, compelled by the tantalizing possibility that the answers to our most profound questions may lie just beyond our current reach. Through rigorous exploration and unyielding inquiry, the marriage of these concepts could ultimately lead us toward unveiling the underlying essence of the cosmos and the fundamental mechanics that govern it.

5.3. Tachyons in a Multiverse

As theories surrounding the multiverse gain traction within cosmological and theoretical physics discussions, the implications of tachyons—as hypothetical particles that could travel faster than light —begin to intersect intriguingly with these expansive models. The multiverse theory posits the existence of parallel universes, each potentially governed by its own physical laws, constants, and spatial-temporal arrangements. Within this rich and complex framework, tachyons introduce profound possibilities for exploring interactions and connections between these different universes.

One implication of tachyons in a multiverse context is the notion that they could serve as conduits or bridging entities between various universes. If tachyons exist and can traverse the speed of light barrier, they may facilitate interactions that seamlessly connect multiple parallel realities. This raises tantalizing questions about the nature of reality itself: could our universe be one of many, shaped and influenced by the passages of superluminal particles that cross the boundaries separating these realms? Such dynamics could enable phenomena currently relegated to the domain of science fiction. For instance, they might allow for the transfer of information or energy between universes, potentially influencing cosmic events in one universe based on interactions occurring in another.

Furthermore, tachyons might provide a conceptual framework for resolving paradoxes typically associated with multiverse theories. Many interpretations of the multiverse grapple with questions of causality, where the branching of alternate realities raises critical doubts about the linearity of time and the continuity of events. However, if tachyons can propagate faster than light, they could shift causal relationships, allowing effects to unfold in one universe as a result of antecedent conditions from another. This perspective challenges classical interpretations of causal sequences and prompts deeper inquiry into how events are interwoven across different domains of existence.

The implications of tachyons extending into a multiverse also touch on the notions of time. The existence of tachyons could redefine our understanding of temporal mechanics; with tachyons, traversing boundaries between universes might challenge our linear perception of time altogether. As superluminal particles facilitate movements across dimensions, they could play a critical role in establishing temporal connections between events in disparate universes, presenting a more fluid and interconnected fabric of time. This revisitation of temporal dynamics opens up intellectual avenues to ponder how time behaves across multiple realities and how we might interpret notions of past, present, and future within such a schema.

The theoretical exploration of multiverses that incorporate tachyons also encourages reflection on the nature of existence itself. Questions arise regarding whether the interactions and influences of tachyons could create detectable effects in our universe that could, in turn, provide evidence for the existence of parallel realities. If tachyons were to traverse the barriers separating different dimensions, they could lead to observable phenomena—perhaps through cosmic anomalies or unexpected interactions within fundamental forces in our own universe—serving as clues pointing toward the existence of a broader multiverse.

Moreover, addressing the philosophical implications of tachyons situates them at the crossroads of science and existential inquiry. The intersection of higher-dimensional physics and the nature of reality, facilitated through the lens of tachyon dynamics, compels us to question what constitutes our understanding of existence. As theorists explore the potential for collaborative interactions among multiple universes via tachyonic behavior, they may unearth new paradigms that deepen our comprehension of our universe's structure, challenging us to reconsider the limitations that govern our conceptual frameworks.

In summary, traversing the landscape of tachyon dynamics within the multiverse framework reveals a myriad of intriguing inquiries and possibilities. As tachyons symbolize nodes of connection, the exploration of their implications in multiple cosmic realities invites a broader and more nuanced understanding of existence itself, time, and the interrelations between potentialities. Ultimately, pondering these connections not only serves scientific pursuits but also enriches philosophical discussions that challenge our long-standing perceptions of the universe, invoking the spirit of exploration fundamental to humanity's quest for knowledge and understanding. The dialogue surrounding tachyons illustrates the extent to which we are willing to journey into speculative realms, where boundaries dissolve and possibilities unveil themselves in the uncharted territories of the cosmos.

5.4. The Big Bang and Forward Time Travel

The exploration of the universe's inception through the lens of tachyons presents a fascinating inquiry that intermingles cosmological theories with the domain of particle physics. At the heart of this discussion lies the mysterious event known as the Big Bang—a moment theorized to have birthed our universe approximately 13.8 billion years ago, marking the beginning of spacetime, matter, and the fundamental forces that govern existence. The implications of tachyons, hypothetical particles posited to travel faster than light, suggest intriguing possibilities regarding their role in shaping the universe during and after this primordial explosion.

To consider whether tachyons could have been influential in the creation of spacetime, we must first understand the conditions that prevailed in the early universe. Initially, the universe was a hot, dense singularity composed of energy in various forms, leading to rapid expansion and cooling. This explosive event laid down the framework for all subsequent cosmic structures, yet many mysteries remain about the nature of forces at play during this critical period. If tachyons were to exist, their superluminal properties could suggest an alternative mechanism for how energy and information were distributed during and right after the Big Bang.

The immediate aftermath of the Big Bang was characterized by extreme temperatures and pressures. Within these conditions, conventional particles may not have functioned as we understand them today. Tachyons—if they exist and were present—might have behaved differently, allowing them to impact the state of the universe in ways we have yet to fully comprehend. Their unique travel properties would imply that they could traverse spacetime constraints, potentially conveying information or influencing interactions in this extremely energetic environment that ordinary particles could not.

Hypothetically, if tachyons were involved in the expansion of the universe, they could act as facilitators of instantaneous communication between disparate regions of the nascent universe. This could mean that, instead of a gradual distribution of energy and matter through interactions limited by the lightspeed barrier, early cosmic events could have unfolded in a manner akin to a synchronous dance orchestrated by the influence of tachyons. In this view, tachyons could lighten the communication burden among the fundamental forces, effectively bridging gaps as the early universe expanded in its chaotic infancy.

When considered within cosmological models, tachyons might elucidate phenomena such as the uniformity observed in the cosmic microwave background radiation, or the astonishingly rapid inflation believed to occur shortly after the Big Bang—a theory suggesting that the universe underwent exponential growth during its early moments. The concept of rapid inflation remains one of the more puzzling aspects of cosmology, primarily due to the discrepancies between expected behavior and observed properties. If tachyons could leverage faster-than-light behavior to exert influence over large distances instantaneously, they might help explain how disparate regions developed uniform characteristics amidst such rapid expansion.

Engaging with these scenarios also invokes deep reflections on the nature of time. The existence of tachyons might challenge our established understanding of temporal mechanics, particularly as we attempt to grapple with events that unfolded in a place where time itself was being forged. If tachyons transcended the boundaries imposed by light speed, could this imply alternative dimensions of temporal existence? Their unique characteristics could invoke philosophical discussions about the nature of existence, reality, and emerging time through the phenomena following the Big Bang—a tantalizing prospect that suggests the birth of the universe was a rich tapestry woven with threads we have yet to fully identify.

However, it is essential to approach these ideas with an understanding of the rigorous standards of scientific inquiry. The existence of tachyons remains hypothetical, and while their proposed characteristics ignite the imagination and enable speculation about their role in cosmological events, empirical evidence is critical to substantiate these claims. Rigorous mathematical modeling and observational studies remain paramount in these explorations, as scientists work diligently to uncover more clues about the mechanisms behind the universe's birth.

In summary, the question of whether tachyons played a role in the creation of spacetime opens a Pandora's box of possibilities that intertwine particle physics with cosmology. Engaging with this inquiry challenges our existing paradigms and urges us to consider how superluminal particles might function within the grand narrative of the universe's formation. As research continues to progress, the dialogue surrounding tachyons can only serve to enrich our understanding by continuing to probe the enigmatic depths of both particle dynamics and cosmic evolution—inviting scientists and philosophers alike to reflect on the very nature of existence and the intricate dance of particles that shapes the cosmos. In this exploration, tachyons stand as a testament to humanity's unyielding quest for comprehension, challenging us to transcend conventional limitations and embrace the manifold possibilities woven into the fabric of reality itself.

5.5. Cosmological Impacts of Tachyon Travel

The cosmological impacts of tachyon travel weave an intricate tapestry of theoretical possibilities that characterize the future of our understanding of the universe. As we consider the implications of hypothetical tachyons, particles theorized to move faster than light, we enter a realm where the boundaries of space and time may become malleable. The very principles that dictate our grasp of cosmic dynamics could undergo profound shifts, leading to potential transformations in how we understand both fundamental physics and the universe at large.

One of the most significant implications of tachyon travel lies in its potential to facilitate interconnectedness across vast cosmic distances. The existence of tachyons could allow for instantaneous communication between disparate regions of the universe, bypassing the light-speed limit set forth by Einstein's theory of relativity. This capability might allow civilizations scattered across the cosmos to exchange information, forming a network of communication that transcends the limitations of conventional technologies. In this speculative scenario, the fabric of the cosmos could serve not merely as a collection of isolated celestial bodies but as an interconnected tapestry of knowledge and inquiry.

Beyond the concept of communication, the incorporation of tachyons into our understanding of cosmology invites us to rethink causative chains within the universe. If tachyons can indeed traverse distances rapidly or exceed the light barrier, the linear progression from cause to effect could become subject to alterations that challenge our conventional understanding of temporal mechanics. For instance, effects that were previously thought to be contingent on their causes may be influenced by tachyonic interactions, suggesting scenarios where causality does not adhere to familiar temporal patterns. This renegotiation of causative sequences could pave the way for exploring new paradigms of reality, inciting philosophical discourse about identity, existence, and the very nature of time.

Tachyon travel might also hold implications for the expansive narrative of cosmic evolution. If these superluminal particles exist and exert influences on the fabric of spacetime, we could witness their impact on various cosmological phenomena, including dark energy and the expansion of the universe itself. The compounds of tachyons could work in concert with existing forces, suggesting that the acceleration of cosmic expansion is underpinned by the dynamics of these elusive entities. Such insights may help clarify unresolved questions regarding the nature of dark energy and the factors driving the universe's continued evolution.

In addition, the transformative potential of tachyon travel evokes intriguing considerations about time itself. With the incorporation of tachyons as part of the cosmic narrative, the arrow of time could shift dramatically. Theability of tachyons to traverse greater-than-light distances could prompt us to rethink the linear flow of time, complicating notions of past, present, and future. If tachyons enable retrocausal interactions—where future events could influence past occurrences—the very essence of our temporal experience may come to reflect a multidimensional panorama of interconnected moments rather than a sequential timeline. These conceptual shifts could reinvigorate discussions around temporal paradoxes, offering resolutions previously thought insurmountable.

As we reflect on the implications of tachyon travel within the cosmos, we must contend with the challenges and criticisms presented by the scientific community. Many physicists remain skeptical about the inherent stability of tachyonic models and their alignment with established physical laws. The speculation surrounding tachyons also raises questions about the validity of their existence in light of existing experimental evidence and understanding of causality. It becomes crucial for proponents of tachyon research to address these concerns through rigorous scrutiny and substantiate their claims with empirical support.

In addition to theoretical considerations, the cosmological impacts of tachyon travel extend into practical domains, encompassing potential applications that reach far beyond today's technological horizons. Advances in communication technology could hinge on the principles of tachyon dynamics, and the dream of instantaneous interstellar communication might transform the very fabric of how we connect with the universe. The pursuit of practical applications stemming from tachyon studies insists on an interdisciplinary dialogue between theoretical physics, engineering, and cosmology—one that continues to propel humanity toward a future defined by coexistence with the cosmos.

Overall, the cosmological impacts of tachyon travel delineate a rich frontier of inquiry that beckons further exploration. By unraveling the implications of hypothetical superluminal particles, we challenge ourselves to reconsider the nature of existence, time, and our connection to the universe. As the pursuit of knowledge continues, the tantalizing possibilities of tachyon travel could illuminate pathways toward deeper understanding, enriching not only the scientific discourse but also the human experience within an ever-expanding cosmic narrative. Through sustained inquiry and open-minded exploration, we may yet unlock the profound mysteries of the universe that lie just beyond our current grasp, inviting us to contemplate the unfathomable wonders that await us among the stars. In this grand odyssey, tachyons symbolize not only theoretical pursuits but humanity's enduring quest for knowledge, beauty, and fundamental truth amid the cosmic expanse.

6. Tachyons and Temporal Mechanics

6.1. The Arrow of Time: Past, Present, and Future

The flow of time, an ever-present dimension affecting all aspects of existence, eludes simple comprehension. We generally perceive time as a linear sequence progressing from past to present to future, a perspective shaped by our day-to-day experiences. However, this traditional understanding may be challenged by the existence of tachyons—hypothetical particles theorized to travel faster than light. The concept of tachyons invites profound questions about the nature of time itself and how it may be perceived and experienced in ways that defy our conventional frameworks.

To understand how tachyons might challenge our linear perception of time, we must first consider the implications of their superluminal velocity. In our current understanding of physics, as established by Einstein's theory of relativity, the speed of light represents a cosmic speed limit for massive particles, with time dilation experienced as one approaches this speed. However, tachyons, by their very nature, would exceed this limit and maintain a unique relationship with time —suggesting the possibility that they could move through time in ways that ordinary particles cannot.

In traditional terms, we experience time as an arrow—conditioned to move in one direction from past to future. If tachyons exist, they may disrupt this arrow by enabling an alternative temporal experience— one in which effects could precede their causes. This notion poses significant implications for causality, as it allows for scenarios where events could be influenced retroactively by future interactions. Such scenarios lead to a reevaluation of the linear sequence we normally associate with time and bear the potential of redefining our understanding of temporal dynamics.

Furthermore, the notion of time itself becomes more complex when considering tachyonic behavior. If we posit tachyons as effective time travelers, moving through temporal dimensions at superluminal speeds, it raises the question of how their presence might simultaneously affect past, present, and future states in our universe. The interactions of tachyons with other particles may create alternate timelines or pathways through time that allow for non-linear interactions across temporal boundaries. This invites organic thoughts about a universe that is not strictly determined by linear progress but is instead a broader tapestry of interwoven events where multiple timelines could coexist.

The implications of superluminal particles extend beyond mere theoretical musings into tangible pathways for interpreting experiences of time. For example, if tachyons can engage in communications or influences across time, time travel might evolve from fiction into a concept grounded in potential scientific reality. As researchers explore the ramifications of tachyonic influences, questions arise about how humanity could harness such phenomena for practical applications—transporting information, knowledge, and even matter across temporal dimensions in ways historically confined to science fiction.

Additionally, if we venture into the philosophy of time in relation to tachyons, we are compelled to investigate whether time may be more appropriately viewed as a multi-dimensional entity rather than a strict one-dimensional flow. The existence of tachyons implies a potential framework in which time itself is interconnected across complexities, allowing for an expansive understanding of temporal relationships. As such, the integration of tachyons into our perception of time could usher forth a transformative paradigm—one in which events unfold not merely along a linear path but also within a multi-dimensional realm.

In summary, tachyons compel us to reconsider the way we perceive time, challenging our instinctual understanding of its linear flow. Their hypothesized qualities open avenues where time may become a vast, interwoven landscape filled with causal relationships that transcend the limitations we currently comprehend. Engaging with the ramifications of tachyons on temporal mechanics not only reverberates through the realm of particle physics but also weaves philosophical inquiries into the intricate tapestry of existence. This exploration serves as a testament to humanity's pursuit of knowledge, constantly reaching into the unknown in a quest to unlock the profound mysteries of time and time travel, while redefining our understanding of ourselves and our universe.

6.2. Temporal Paradoxes and Tachyon Solutions

Temporal paradoxes present one of the most intriguing challenges in theoretical physics, particularly within discussions surrounding time travel. These paradoxes, often illustrated by classic thought experiments such as the grandfather paradox, prompt essential questions about causality, the linearity of time, and the very nature of existence. As we delve into the dynamics of tachyons—hypothetical particles theorized to travel faster than light—we uncover potential solutions to these paradoxes that stretch the boundaries of conventional understanding.

At the heart of a temporal paradox lies the contradiction that arises when cause and effect are called into question. For instance, if one were to travel back in time and inadvertently prevent their own existence—by, for example, stopping one's grandparents from meeting—the question arises: if the time traveler never existed, how could they have traveled back in time in the first place? This self-referential loop creates a logical inconsistency that challenges the very framework of causality.

Tachyons offer a unique perspective on these convoluted scenarios. If tachyons exist and can traverse time and space at superluminal speeds, they might possess properties that allow them to circumvent traditional causality constraints. In this context, tachyons could introduce a new dimension of causal relationships—one that permits the existence of events occurring without adhering to the linear structure of cause followed by effect.

Consider a theoretical model in which a tachyonic signal is sent back in time to communicate with the past, potentially influencing events that could lead to paradoxical outcomes. Encountering a tachyonic particle might allow information to propagate instantaneously across temporal boundaries, creating a scenario where an event in the future impacts the past without necessarily creating a causal loop. This superluminal transition could introduce alternate timelines or branching realities, where different outcomes unfold concurrently rather than contradicting the linearity of time.

In this framework, the very act of sending a tachyon back in time could seed alternative universes rather than collapse the timeline into contradiction. The existence of tachyons could be conceptualized as not just a means of navigating through time, but also as agents of change that populate a multiverse—a collection of possible realities where divergent outcomes based on the same initial conditions coexist. Rather than posing a single, contradictory timeline, tachyons might facilitate a multitude of pathways, allowing events to unfold in various contexts, each representing a unique reality.

Furthermore, the application of tachyonic dynamics on temporal mechanics invites recalibrating our understanding of how time itself is structured. In this perspective, events may not simply follow a linear flow but could interact in a complex web wherein precedence is not universally guaranteed. Causality, in the presence of tachyons, would therefore require a reimagining—enabling effects not confined to causative sequences and allowing time to become a more fluid framework.

The ramifications of such theoretical models extend far beyond paradox resolution. The implications of tachyon theory on time travel resonate throughout both scientific inquiry and philosophical discourse. If tachyons can adequately address temporal paradoxes, they could open avenues for exploring advanced concepts such as retrocausality, where future outcomes influence the past. This would redefine our understanding of time travel and challenge the fundamental assumptions that govern our perception of existence.

Moreover, addressing temporal paradoxes through tachyons interacts harmoniously with broader discussions around the nature of time itself. Viewing time as a multi-dimensional construct aligns with theories that posit time as a more complex, non-linear phenomenon. Such a view acknowledges that while we may perceive time with a forward trajectory, its intrinsic qualities—the interconnectedness of events, the interplay of past and future—may resemble a rich tapestry rather than a simple chronological line.

In conclusion, while traditional perspectives struggle with the complexities posed by temporal paradoxes, the introduction of tachyons into these discussions revitalizes the dialogue. By envisioning superluminal particles as agents capable of transcending the constraints of casual limits, we not only devise potential solutions to paradoxical scenarios but also challenge prevailing notions about the very fabric of time. As this exploration continues, we may yet find ourselves at the precipice of a new understanding of existence—one wherein the foundations of causality and temporality harmoniously intertwine, yielding insights that reshape our grasp of the universe.

6.3. Causality and Time Travel Theories

Causality, the principle that dictates the relationship between events as causes and effects, occupies a central place in our comprehension of time and physical laws. The intersection of this principle with theories of time travel, particularly through the lens of tachyons— hypothetical particles purported to traverse faster than light—opens a Pandora's box of paradoxes and potential resolutions that challenge our conventional understanding of reality.

The advent of tachyon theory invites a reevaluation of causality in light of superluminal motion. If these particles exist and indeed transmit information or signals at speeds exceeding that of light, we confront scenarios contravening our standard temporal frameworks. In classical physics, causality assumes a linear progression, where causes lead to effects in a sequential manner. However, introducing tachyons into this narrative hints at the possibility of non-linear time travel, where future events might impact past ones, effectively challenging the very notion that the past is immutable.

This rethinking of temporal dynamics finds resonance in hypothetical scenarios often illustrated by the classic grandfather paradox. In such a scenario, if a time traveler were able to traverse back in time and prevent a pivotal event—such as their grandparents meeting—the logical conclusion draws attention to a contradiction: if the time traveler alters past events, they negate their own existence in the future. Such paradoxes converge beautifully with tachyon dynamics, which could facilitate alternative resolutions. For instance, tachyons could enable oversight in a universe that accommodates branching timelines, positing that the time traveler creates a new reality wherein their original timeline persists independently.

These speculative ideas raise significant queries about whether tachyons might serve as conduits capable of navigating complex temporal paths without incurring paradoxical consequences. Rather than reverting to a limiting view where time unfolds linearly from past to future, we can conceptualize a multidimensional framework where events intertwine, influenced by superluminal interactions. In this view, causative chains could exist as a network, allowing more fluid associations between past and future without rendering paradoxes.

Moreover, viewing tachyons through the lens of causality positions us to reconsider the fundamental structure of time itself. Could time be less about uniform progression and more about interwoven experiences that allow influence across dimensions? If tachyons enable instantaneous connections, the experiencing of events could occur simultaneously in a larger cosmic tapestry—inviting a provocative reconfiguration of our understanding of existence.

As we examine the relationship between tachyons and causality, we must grapple with the epistemological implications of such interactions. The pursuit of evidence supporting tachyon dynamics encourages rigorous inquiry into the nature of reality, invoking questions about our perceptions of time and how they shape our lived experiences. While these ideas may sound speculative, they hold potent implications for scientific advancement—particularly in understanding theoretical constructs of time travel and the nature of the cosmos.

In advancing the discussion about tachyons and causality, we embrace the complexities inherent in this dialogue, where traditional dogmas begin to unravel, waiting to be reconstructed into a more coherent and profound understanding of existence. As researchers explore the ramifications of these particles, we stand on the cusp of a broadly enriched comprehension of time, employing the principles of tachyons to move past simple contradictions and toward a more complex, integrated view of reality. Consequently, engaging with these theories challenges not only our scientific paradigms but also the philosophical musings that underpin humanity's innermost inquiries about existence.

6.4. Are Tachyons the Key to Avoiding Time Loops?

To understand the potential of tachyons in avoiding time loops, we must first recognize the implications of time travel as portrayed in both popular culture and scientific theory. The challenge with time travel lies in the paradoxes it often presents—foremost among them, the troubling concept of the "time loop" or causal loop. In standard narratives, these loops create scenarios where the future causes events in the past, fundamentally contradicting our intuitive understanding of causality. Here, tachyons, the postulated superluminal particles, might provide the key to navigating these complex webs of temporal contradiction.

Time loops pose significant philosophical and physical dilemmas. Within a causal loop, actions taken in the future are instrumental to shaping past events, leading to circular dependencies that defy logical reasoning. For example, a time traveler might go back to ensure an event occurs but inadvertently causes their own existence or the initial time travel itself. The question that arises is: if a character performs an action in one time frame only to produce the condition that allowed them to time travel in the first place, what does this mean for their agency and the linear progression of events?

Tachyons, with their purported ability to traverse faster than light, could offer a crucial perspective in understanding and potentially avoiding these paradoxical entanglements. If we consider tachyons as particles that operate outside the traditional limits imposed by spacetime, they may afford a means for information exchange that redefines the parameters of potential causality. Instead of propagating a straightforward cause leading to an effect, the presence of tachyons in a time travel scenario might enable a system where signals or influences can exist simultaneously across distinct temporal planes, circumventing the rigid chains of causation typically depicted in time-travel narratives.

Imagine a scenario wherein a tachyon is utilized as a messenger or mediator of information across time. Instead of a time traveler encountering their past self and creating a contradiction, the interaction facilitated through tachyonic influence could result in non-linear effects—effects able to coexist without imposing the circular logic of time loops. For example, a future tachyonic signal could influence an event in the past while simultaneously preserving multiple outcomes and timelines—effectively disentangling the entrapment of one possible future causing its own past.

This mechanism aligns with our understanding of quantum mechanics, wherein particles display behaviors that defy classical interpretations. Just as quantum entanglement allows for instantaneous influences over distances, tachyons could weave a network of informational influence across the fragile fabric of time itself. Rather than relying on a linear temporal chain, the relationships established by tachyons could contribute to a more intricate timeline characterized by various possible futures—each deriving distinct threads from mutual past experiences.

Moreover, introducing tachyons into time travel theories may provide insights that alter our perspectives on the nature of time itself. If tachyons could allow actions to resonate across time in a more fluid manner, time might not appear as an unbending arrow, as traditionally conceived, but rather as a vibrating tableau that accommodates multiple realities and timelines coexisting. This fluidity could serve to offer potential resolutions to not only paradoxes but also enhance our comprehension of existence and interaction through temporal dimensions.

However, several hurdles remain if we wish to apply tachyons as a solution to temporal loops. First and foremost, the lack of empirical evidence for tachyon existence complicates their theoretical applications. The speculative nature of their properties means that much work remains to be done to create a coherent theoretical framework. Additionally, researchers must unravel the complexities of tachyon dynamics and causal relationships in order to solidify their applications in theoretical and experimental constructs.

In summary, tachyons present a captivating avenue of exploration in the realm of time travel and temporal mechanics. By theorizing the effects of superluminal particles, researchers can begin to conceive of mechanisms that allow us to circumvent the contradictions intrinsic to time loops—that challenge the very nature of our understanding of causation. Engaging with these ideas not only enriches our scientific discussions but also uplifts the narratives we craft around time, existence, and the boundless curiosity that propels humanity's quest for knowledge beyond the stars. The potential for tachyons to play a significant role in reshaping our interactions with time compels us to continue our inquiries, inviting us to explore realms that defy our current understanding of reality itself.

6.5. Viewing Time as a Dimension

The concept of time as a dimension has evolved significantly in the landscape of modern physics, particularly with the advent of theories exploring the nature of tachyons—hypothetical particles theorized to move faster than light. To comprehend the intricate relationship between time and tachyons, we must challenge our traditional understanding of time as merely a linear progression of events and instead view it as a multifaceted dimension interwoven with the fabric of spacetime.

In classical physics, time is often perceived as a distinct entity that progresses uniformly, serving as a backdrop against which events unfold. This perspective, however, fails to encapsulate the complexities introduced by both Einstein's theory of relativity and the emerging frameworks of quantum mechanics. As we probe deeper into the nature of tachyons, their implications encourage us to redefine our conceptualization of time itself.

Einstein's theory of relativity fundamentally restructured our understanding of time, introducing the idea that it is not an absolute construct but rather intertwined with space to form a four-dimensional continuum known as spacetime. Within this framework, time varies according to the observer's relative motion and gravitational field, revealing a dimension that is flexible, influenced by the very nature of the universe itself. For example, as objects approach the speed of light, time dilates, leading to phenomena like twin paradoxes, where one twin traveling at relativistic speeds ages more slowly than their stationary counterpart.

Tachyons, in this context, introduce additional dimensions to our understanding of time. Hypothetically possessing imaginary mass, tachyons, if they exist, would move faster than light and could even enjoy a unique relationship with temporal mechanics. Imaging tachyons existing in a superluminal state opens the door to the notion that they may experience time differently compared to massy particles. Where conventional particles follow a linear timeline dictated by causality, tachyons might traverse distances and time in a manner where their very nature distorts the traditional characteristics of time.

If we entertain the idea of tachyonic travel, it encourages new interpretations of causality and time's arrow—the principle that causes precede their effects. Superluminal motion could lead to scenarios where effects precede their causes, fundamentally disrupting our linear narrative of time. This invites a potentially radical understanding of the universe, where events can occur in unexpected sequences and timelines can branch into multiple outcomes.

Moreover, introducing tachyons influences philosophical inquiries surrounding the nature of time. If these particles can move through time in ways that challenge conventional boundaries, it compels us to think of time as a more interconnected, fluid construct rather than a rigid sequence. In this multi-dimensional understanding, the past and future may not be discrete entities but part of a continuum influenced by interactions across various states of existence.

Exploring the implications of tachyons on time also aligns with discourse around quantum mechanics, particularly in light of phenomena such as quantum entanglement. If tachyons can facilitate instantaneous connections across vast distances or time, they open dialogues about how interactions across the fabric of reality may reshape our comprehension of speed and existence.

In summary, viewing time as a dimension in the context of tachyons forces us to recalibrate our understanding of the universe, transcending the limits of our traditional perceptions. It beckons us to contemplate the complexities of existence, the nature of causality, and the potential realities that emerge within the interplay of time and particle dynamics. By embracing these contemplations, we are increasingly drawn into a multifaceted exploration of the cosmos—where time, space, and everything in between are imbued with deeper meanings waiting to be unveiled. As we continue to investigate the properties of tachyons and their implications for time, we may find ourselves at the forefront of a new epoch in our quest for knowledge, compelled to rethink our relationship with the very essence of existence itself.

7. The Evidence Spectrum: From Theory to Experiment

7.1. Laboratory Tests: Practical Pursuits

Efforts to produce or detect tachyons in controlled settings represent a significant frontier in experimental physics, where the boundaries of theoretical speculation intersect with the practicality of laboratory research. The quest to confirm the existence of tachyons demands rigorous methodologies and innovative experimental designs that both honor the foundational principles of physics while daring to challenge the known limitations of the universe.

Central to the endeavor of detecting tachyons is the development of experimental frameworks that can operate within the constraints of current technology and understanding. One proposed method involves high-energy particle collisions, akin to those conducted at large particle accelerators like the Large Hadron Collider (LHC). In these experiments, particles are accelerated to energies approaching the speed of light, creating conditions ripe for exploring the resulting interactions. Theoretically, should tachyons exist, their interactions could generate observable signatures—a unique emission pattern or trace that distinguishes them from other known particles. Scientists might analyze end products of these collisions, seeking anomalies that align with tachyonic behaviors, particularly signatures that indicate superluminal velocities or the presence of imaginary mass.

Another potential avenue for tachyon detection lies in the analysis of cosmic rays—high-energy particles that bombarded the Earth from space. If tachyons indeed traverse spacetime with superluminal characteristics, then it stands to reason that such particles could manifest through unexplained changes in cosmic ray trajectories or unexpected energy spikes. Amateur astronomers, physicists, and cosmologists might collaborate to telescope into the sky for cosmic events that resonate with the expected outcomes of tachyon interactions, seeking anomalies in cosmic background radiation that might provide clues regarding their existence.

Experimental approaches must also contend with the highly speculative nature of tachyon theory itself. This entails a keen awareness of the existing limitations of our measurement technologies and theoretical frameworks. For instance, the portrayal of tachyons as imaginary mass particles introduces significant challenges, as any observational models need to reconcile such a characteristic with existing understandings of physical interactions. Additionally, the ramifications of relativity complicate the search; as the speed of light serves as a cosmological speed limit for massive particles, discerning tachyonic interactions from ordinary particle behaviors without yielding false positives requires meticulous attention to detail.

Practical tests also underscore the importance of interdisciplinary collaboration between physicists, engineers, and computer scientists. Advanced data analysis techniques—perhaps incorporating machine learning algorithms—can augment the ability to parse complex datasets generated from high-energy collisions or cosmic ray impacts. This sophisticated analysis is critical in filtering out noise and identifying anomalous patterns that potentially signal tachyonic behavior.

An essential component of any experimental physicist's approach is the peer review process, which serves as a mechanism for rigorously evaluating proposed tachyon detection methodologies. This scrutiny invites critical feedback that can refine elements of experimental design and enhance the robustness of findings. By juxtaposing multiple approaches across diverse research institutions, scientists can cultivate a more diverse and comprehensive understanding of tachyons' potential existence.

Ultimately, the pursuit of laboratory tests for tachyons encapsulates the essence of scientific inquiry—a venture filled with curiosity, rigor, and the willingness to test the boundaries of established knowledge. While the challenges are substantial, the potential revelations that may emerge from these experimental endeavors could revolutionize our understanding of physics and the nature of reality itself.

As the scientific community remains vigilant in its quest for empirical evidence, the possibilities that tachyons represent remain tantalizingly within reach. The historical context of groundbreaking discoveries in physics suggests that by daring to explore the speculative aspects of tachyon research, we may unveil profound truths that redefine our comprehension of the universe. This endeavor stands not only as a journey into the unknown but as a testament to humanity's enduring drive to transcend constraints in the search for knowledge and understanding of our existence amidst the cosmos.

7.2. Astrophysical Evidence: Searching the Stars

The exploration for astrophysical evidence of tachyons shifts our focus beyond terrestrial confines, prompting us to contemplate cosmic phenomena that may suggest the existence of these enigmatic superluminal particles. As scientists broaden their inquiries across the vast expanse of the universe, searching for insights that might lend credence to tachyon theory begins to take on multiple dimensions. This inquiry encompasses theoretical predictions, observational data, and indirect indicators that could inform our understanding of both the cosmos and the principles governing the nature of speed, time, and causality.

One compelling avenue of exploration arises from the examination of cosmic rays—high-energy particles originating from astronomical sources that bombard Earth from all directions. These energetic phenomena, primarily consisting of protons and atomic nuclei, present a potential venue for discovering signatures that hint at tachyonic behavior. Researchers have speculated that if tachyons exist, they may interact with cosmic rays in ways that deviate from conventional predictions, giving rise to unexpected collision patterns, energy distributions, or anomalous trajectories. Detecting such deviations among cosmic rays could serve as indirect evidence of tachyonic influences within the universe, prompting deeper investigations into their characteristics.

In tandem with cosmic rays, the study of gamma-ray bursts (GRBs) constitutes another exciting frontier in the quest for tachyonic evidence. GRBs represent the most luminous events observed in the universe, often associated with the collapse of massive stars or the merger of neutron stars. The rapidly varying nature of these explosions inspires inquiry into whether tachyons might play a role in propagating energy across cosmic distances instantaneously, preserving the coherence of emitted gamma radiation. If tachyons were indeed involved in the mechanisms driving these extraordinary events, we might expect to uncover unique patterns of energy release or decay rates that align with theoretical tachyonic predictions.

Additionally, the frameworks provided by quantum gravity theories suggest another potential avenue for leanings toward tachyons in the universe. Work within these marginal realms, including string theory and loop quantum gravity, often grapples with reconciling relativity with quantum mechanics and presents models where superluminal particles exist. Though deeply theoretical, such frameworks beckon serious consideration for experimental astrophysics, propelling inquiries into high-energy cosmic phenomena that could hint at tachyonic intertwining within the universe's digital tapestry.

Gravitational waves, another captivating aspect of modern astrophysical study, may add further layers to our understanding. In the wake of the groundbreaking discovery of gravitational waves, physicists are now investigating their implications for various physical phenomena. As tachyons—if they exist—are theorized to interact differently with spacetime, their presence may affect the gravitational wave patterns observable as ripples in spacetime produced by astronomical occurrences. A search for patterns linking gravitational waves and superluminal particles presents a potential area for further empirical inquiry.

The scrutiny extends beyond direct cosmic observations. Astrophysical phenomena that remain poorly understood, such as dark matter and dark energy, have invoked speculation surrounding tachyon interactions, prompting researchers to seek connections between these enigmatic components and potential tachyonic influences. Understanding the interplay of these forces could lend insights into the fundamental structure of the universe—a context where tachyons might dwell as agents of change.

Continuing our exploration, the statistical analysis of large astronomical datasets holds promise. As technology advances and observational astronomy generates vast amounts of data, researchers can apply sophisticated algorithms and machine learning to sift through the noise, seeking out anomalies that align with tachyon predictions. Each unexpected correlation may bear witness to phenomena that hint at the existence of tachyons, urging scientists to reassess established models and expand theoretical frameworks.

However, the pursuit of astrophysical evidence is not without challenges. The inherently speculative nature of tachyon theory often leads to skepticism from the scientific community—rooted in the stringent requirements of empirical validation and the necessity to rely on established scientific principles. The absence of direct methods to isolate tachyons complicates observational pursuits, underscoring the importance of maintaining rigorous standards of inquiry while remaining open to creative exploration beyond established scientific confines.

In conclusion, the search for tachyons through astrophysical evidence unfurls a rich tapestry of inquiry that bridges theoretical predictions with cosmic observations. By examining cosmic rays, gamma-ray bursts, gravitational waves, and other enigmatic phenomena, scientists open doors to the possibility of confirming tachyon existence. This journey encourages collaboration among fields—including theoretical physics, astrophysics, and data science—in pursuit of elusive truths that may revolutionize our understanding of the universe. Ultimately, the quest for tachyons embodies humanity's relentless curiosity to explore the cosmos, unveiling the secrets nestled within the fabric of existence itself.

7.3. Challenges in Experimental Physics

Experimental physics faces a multitude of challenges, particularly when it comes to the theoretical exploration of tachyons—hypothetical particles that, if they exist, would possess the extraordinary ability to travel faster than light. Addressing these challenges requires meticulous scientific inquiry, innovative thinking, and a willingness to navigate the complex interplay between theoretical models and empirical validation.

Firstly, one of the primary obstacles lies in the inherently speculative nature of tachyons. As theoretical constructs, proposed to possess imaginary mass and exhibit superluminal velocities, their existence remains unproven. Most experimental efforts in physics are built on established principles with solid empirical backing, leading to skepticism about any pursuits concerning tachyons. When scientists engage in exploring phenomena grounded in speculative theory, they confront the daunting challenge of framing experimental designs that align with existing knowledge while accommodating the bold deviations that tachyon theory entails.

This skepticism leads directly to another significant challenge: the lack of a clear methodology for detection. Unlike particles such as electrons or protons, which can be manipulated and examined in controlled environments, tachyons, with their imagined properties, resist straightforward detection. The experiments designed to uncover their existence must contend with complex variables, such as the unpredictable nature of high-energy collisions and interactions that are often fraught with noise from background effects. To seek out tachyons, researchers must craft experiments that differentiate between normal particle behaviors and any anomalies that might suggest superluminal activity, all while operating under the stringent standards governing experimental physics.

Building upon this challenge, we find that high-energy particle experiments, while promising, require immense resources, sophisticated technology, and interdisciplinary collaboration. Facilities like the Large Hadron Collider facilitate these inquiries, yet the vast data generated needs to be carefully analyzed. The filtering of noise and accurately interpreting the results from such experiments are non-trivial tasks that necessitate advanced data analytics techniques—an area that demands both expertise and innovation in computational approaches. Moreover, the investment into such large-scale experimental designs underscores the risk inherent in pursuing speculative theories that may ultimately yield inconclusive results.

As discussions around tachyons expand, experimental physicists are also confronted with philosophical issues surrounding causality and the foundational principles of physics. Tachyons introduce counter-intuitive implications regarding the relationships between events in spacetime, leading to doubts about the viability of their existence within a conventional scientific framework. Many physicists remain firmly committed to Einstein's theories of relativity and may resist the challenge posed to their rigor, further complicating collaborative efforts to advance tachyon research.

Moreover, the scattered nature of funding in scientific research often places speculative fields like tachyon studies at a disadvantage compared to more established disciplines. Support for inquiry into areas with wider recognition and immediate application—like condensed matter physics or materials science—can overshadow more theoretical pursuits. Consequently, securing the resources needed for extensive research into tachyons presents an ongoing hurdle that researchers must navigate.

The lack of empirical data also plays a critical role in shaping public perceptions of tachyons and contributes to the challenges faced by experimental physicists. While public fascination with the concept of faster-than-light travel is undeniable, the disparity between popular science and rigorous scholarly inquiry can create conceptual friction. Misunderstandings breed skepticism from funding bodies, leading to a reluctance to invest in speculative research, even when compelling theoretical models warrant exploration.

However, approaching these challenges requires a dual commitment to scientific rigor and imaginative speculation. When facing the roadblocks within the investigation of tachyons, physicists are tasked with operating at the intersection of discovery and innovation. Developing targeted research that integrates cutting-edge technology, theoretical refinement, and the willingness to engage with philosophical implications characterizes a path forward.

In closing, the challenges faced in the pursuit of understanding tachyons reveal a rich landscape that embodies the complexities of experimental physics. While the hurdles are manifold—ranging from theoretical uncertainty to experimental feasibility—the impulse to explore the boundaries of knowledge persists. Through tenacity, collaborative engagement, and creative problem-solving, researchers may ultimately forge pathways to uncover profound truths about the universe, the nature of time, and the tantalizing concept of superluminal travel. This pursuit not only signifies the quest for scientific understanding but also reflects the enduring human drive to unravel the mysteries woven deeply into the fabric of existence.

7.4. Results to Date: A Scientific Analysis

The empirical exploration of tachyons has garnered a great deal of interest, reflecting ongoing debates within the scientific community regarding the existence and implications of these hypothetical superluminal particles. Despite the fact that direct evidence of tachyons remains elusive, a growing body of theoretical models and experimental inquiries have emerged, stimulating discussion surrounding possible avenues toward validation.

To date, the most notable efforts have centered around high-energy physics experiments, particularly at large particle colliders like the Large Hadron Collider (LHC). These facilities are designed to accelerate particles to relativistic speeds and facilitate collisions that can probe the limits of our current understanding of particle physics. Theoretically, if tachyons exist, their interactions may yield unique patterns or signatures in the aftermath of particle collisions—signatures that would deviate from expected behaviors exhibited by known particles. Researchers have employed sophisticated data analysis techniques to comb through vast arrays of collision data, looking for anomalies that might indicate superluminal interactions.

However, tracing tachyons through standard detection methods has proven challenging, primarily due to their imagined properties—particularly the concept of imaginary mass. This characteristic complicates predictions regarding how tachyons might generate observable effects within established frameworks. The question thus arises: can physicists derive observable consequences from theoretical predictions pertaining to tachyons in a discernible manner? To bridge this gap, various model scenarios are explored, considering tachyon interactions and their influence on the established physics landscape.

Moreover, astrophysical phenomena offer an intriguing context for potential evidence of tachyon behavior. The study of cosmic rays, gamma-ray bursts, and even gravitational waves prompts consideration of whether signs of tachyonic influence can be discovered in the patterns of these remarkable events. For instance, unexpected fluctuations in cosmic ray intensity or energy distributions might suggest superluminal activity, offering indirect support for tachyon theory. Similarly, an investigation into how gravitational waves might interact with hypothetical tachyonic entities poses a frontier for future astrophysical research, where tachyons could play a role in shaping cosmic events.

Across the scientific literature, theoretical models have expanded, reinforcing various elements of tachyon theories while acknowledging the sobering distance from experimental confirmation. Constructs rooted in quantum field theory have been proposed, suggesting how integrating tachyons into existing frameworks could yield insights into fundamental components of the universe—dark matter and dark energy being among the most tantalizing. The coupling of tachyon models with these elusive components could lead to sophisticated interpretations that broaden the horizon of our understanding in areas where conventional methods have thus far fallen short.

As investigations continue, critiques emerge from skeptics who question the validity of pursuing tachyon research without concrete empirical support. Critics argue that the theoretical inconsistencies inherent in tachyon models serve as an impediment to their acceptance within mainstream physics. Consequently, a healthy debate ensues, continuously challenging the scientific community to refine its methodologies and contextualize findings within broader frameworks.

In summary, while tangible evidence of tachyons remains unverified, the spectrum of inquiry spans both theoretical and experimental realms, yielding meaningful discussions surrounding their potential implications. The quest for empirical data continues to evolve, encouraging scientists to explore the boundaries of known physics while remaining grounded in the pursuit of rigorous scientific inquiry. Future research endeavors will undoubtedly push the frontiers of our understanding, shedding light on whether tachyons are a mere byproduct of theoretical speculation or if they represent a genuine aspect of the universe's intricate tapestry. The ongoing dialogue that emerges from these explorations underscores the dynamic nature of scientific discourse, where curiosity, skepticism, and innovative exploration coalesce to illuminate the cosmic mysteries that persist beyond our current grasp.

7.5. Potential Breakthroughs on the Horizon

In a realm of scientific exploration, the possibility of tachyons—hypothetical particles theorized to surpass the speed of light—stands at the forefront, embodying both audacious imagination and intellectual rigor. As researchers delve deeper into quantum mechanics, relativity, and astrophysical phenomena, a myriad of potential breakthroughs loom on the horizon, urging a reconsideration of our understanding of both time and the very fabric of reality. Over the coming years, these exciting advancements may reshape not only theoretical physics but could also usher in practical implications across various fields.

One of the most ambitious endeavors already in motion is the candid examination of quantum field theories in which tachyons could inherently exist. By refining models that incorporate superluminal particles, physicists can hypothesize new forms of interactions and symmetries that challenge traditional quantum paradigms. Research groups across the globe are actively seeking to draft mathematical formulations that align tachyon theories with established frameworks, such as string theory or quantum gravity, thereby increasing the potential for discovering empirical evidence that could affirm their existence.

High-energy particle colliders, like the Large Hadron Collider (LHC) and potential future facilities, represent hotbeds of exploration where researchers probe the fundamental limits of our understanding of particle physics. These cutting-edge facilities aim to investigate not only known particles but also anomalies that may suggest the interactions of tachyons. Innovative measurement technologies are being developed to better analyze collisions, enhance data resolution, and isolate signals that may hint at superluminal interactions. Notably, ongoing advancements in machine learning and data mining techniques present avenues for scientists to discern tachyonic signatures amidst the vast datasets generated by experiments, potentially leading to groundbreaking discoveries.

Astrophysical observation remains another frontier ripe with opportunity. Researchers are actively scrutinizing cosmic phenomena, including cosmic rays and the behaviors of gamma-ray bursts, searching for any signs that align with tachyonic predictions. For instance, certain cosmic events—characterized by unexpected energy distributions—might reveal anomalous behaviors indicating tachyon interactions. Continuously monitoring and analyzing these phenomena could yield vital clues, igniting a newfound interest in understanding how tachyons might influence universal dynamics.

Moreover, theoretical physicists are exploring the implications of tachyons for cosmological models and the nature of dark matter and dark energy. Innovative approaches may propose tachyonic interactions as essential elements contributing to the accelerated expansion of the universe. By integrating tachyon dynamics into existing frameworks, physicists can illuminate aspects of cosmic phenomena that remain obscured. This avenue holds tremendous promise for enriching our understanding of the universe's composition and fundamentally altering our conception of fundamental forces.

Possibilities in technology also abound, as concepts surrounding tachyonic phenomena inspire speculative engineering designs. Future developments could lead to novel propulsion systems that harness tachyon interactions, facilitating interstellar travel at unprecedented speeds. While these ideas may seem farfetched today, they reflect humanity's enduring curiosity and relentless innovation, reminding us that the boundary between science fiction and reality is often more permeable than we might assume.

Finally, the pursuit of tachyon research could catalyze a new generation of scientists entering the fields of theoretical and experimental physics. As curiosity about superluminal particles ignites imaginations, educators and mentors will play a pivotal role in guiding aspiring researchers toward careers in this fascinating domain. By nurturing enthusiasm in this dynamically evolving field, we can ensure that bright minds will rise to confront the mysteries of the cosmos, pushing the boundaries of knowledge forward.

In conclusion, the prospects for tachyon research stretch beyond tantalizing theoretical implications; they represent the confluence of scientific inquiry, innovation, and philosophical exploration. As researchers embark on the quest to unlock the enigmas surrounding tachyons, they not only challenge the prevailing boundaries of physics but also pave the way for transformative breakthroughs capable of reshaping our understanding of time, space, and existence itself. The next few years promise rich discoveries and a deeper understanding of the cosmos, beckoning keen minds to join the quest to unveil the hidden truths that may lie just beyond the confines of our current reality.

8. The Skeptics: Criticism and Debate

8.1. The Limits of Physical Law: A Critique

The proposition of tachyons—hypothetical particles posited to move faster than light—strikes at the very heart of contemporary physics, compelling a reevaluation of established scientific paradigms. While tachyons incite intrigue and generate animated discussions among enthusiasts and theorists alike, they also elicit skepticism from various quarters of the scientific community. This critique explores the limitations of physical law as it pertains to the existence of tachyons, reflecting the hesitance and criticism from well-established scientific principles.

To commence, the cornerstone of modern physics is predicated on the framework established by Einstein's theory of relativity, which notably enshrines the speed of light as the ultimate cosmic speed limit. This principle affirms that no physical object possessing mass can reach or exceed the speed of light without requiring infinite energy, thus safeguarding established conservation laws. Tachyons, by definition, would undermine this foundational pillar of contemporary physics by necessitating a fundamental reconsideration of mass-energy dynamics. Moreover, the concept of imaginary mass —attributed to tachyons—exposes contradictions that challenge the very validity of existing physical laws.

Critics argue that the introduction of tachyons raises more questions than it resolves, particularly regarding causality. The speculative nature of superluminal travel implies that effects could precede their causes in a tachyon-interactive universe. This notion disturbs the linear conception of time and causation that defines much of classical physics. It invites paradoxical scenarios that conflict not just with relativity but with the intuitive understanding of temporal and causal relationships. Were tachyons to exist and engage in interactions that permit retrocausality, it could lead to logical inconsistencies—similar to the well-known grandfather paradox. The existence of paradoxes challenges the scientific endeavor to maintain coherent and logical frameworks and raises concerns about the epistemological underpinnings of science itself.

The skepticism surrounding superluminal particles is also grounded in the absence of empirical evidence supporting tachyon dynamics. Despite extensive theoretical inquiry, no compelling experimental results have been reported that offer even the slightest indication of tachyons or similar phenomena. The scientific method, reliant on repeatable and observable evidence, renders mere theoretical speculation insufficient in the pursuit of acceptance within the scientific community. In rare instances, proposals have surfaced to illustrate potential avenues for detective endeavors—such as analyzing cosmic rays or employing particle colliders—but these ventures have yet to yield any definitive evidence of tachyons under existing experimental paradigms.

Furthermore, the integration of tachyons into established theoretical frameworks has encountered significant resistance. The effort to harmonize hypothetical particles with the principles of quantum mechanics and general relativity has proven arduous. Many physicists view the link between tachyons and existing models as a convoluted attempt to uphold theoretical constructs without adequate substantiation. Thus, attempts to incorporate tachyons are often labeled as speculative ventures straying from the rigor essential to scientific discourse.

Another aspect that generates skepticism revolves about the attractive allure of tachyons, which, while appealing to the imagination and the fascination with time travel, may present a risk of veering into the realm of pseudoscience. In an age where extraordinary claims often capture public interest and find their way into popular culture, the discourse surrounding tachyons faces the potential for misuse or misrepresentation. Scientists are wary of having their inquiries conflated with pseudoscientific narratives, urging ongoing vigilance against conflating true scientific exploration with sensationalist portrayals.

Despite this skepticism, one of the strengths of scientific discourse lies in its healthy debate. Engaging with dissenting views fosters deeper player understanding—highlighting the complexities of tachyon theories while refining the standards upon which scientific inquiry is built. Debates surrounding tachyons propel researchers to confront their assumptions, recalibrate their methodologies, and draw from diverse perspectives to collectively nurture scientific understanding. This constructive dialogue serves not only to clarify the limitations of tachyon theories but also reinforces the foundational values that underpin the scientific process: scrutiny, skepticism, and inquiry through evidence-based methodologies.

In conclusion, the critique of tachyons emphasizes the limits of physical law that define our understanding of the universe while engaging with the ongoing debates surrounding their potential existence. This discourse serves both as a reminder that speculative ideas must yield to empirical validation and as an acknowledgment of the ceaseless human curiosity to penetrate the unknown. The scientific pursuit of knowledge continues to thrive within a landscape marked by both enthusiasm for innovative possibilities and the disciplined rigor necessary to assess those very possibilities critically. As we navigate this complex terrain, we honor the mathematical and conceptual frameworks robustly established while remaining ever vigilant to explore the enigmatic realms that still await exploration.

8.2. Philosophical Counterarguments

As we delve into the philosophical counterarguments surrounding the concept of tachyons and their implications for superluminal travel, it becomes clear that the discourse extends beyond the confines of pure physics into the realm of metaphysical inquiry. These discussions prompt us to reflect critically on the very nature of existence, causality, and the fundamental structure of reality as we understand it.

Philosophically, tachyons challenge our intuitions about time and causality, raising questions that echo throughout history. The notion that a particle might traverse distances faster than light implies a rethinking of established temporal frameworks. If tachyons indeed exist and possess the ability to violate the cosmic speed limit established by Einstein's theory of relativity, what does this mean for our understanding of cause and effect? Traditional views posit that effects must follow their causes in a linear and temporal hierarchy; however, tachyons could introduce scenarios where the future influences the past—creating non-linear time loops that defy common sense.

Such implications lead to a tapestry of philosophical dilemmas, including the fatalistic notions that may arise from retrocausality. If the future could dictate past events, does it suggest that our actions are predetermined? This circularity brings forth a host of questions regarding free will and responsibility. The notion that our decisions today may be influenced by yet-to-occur events fundamentally alters our understanding of agency within a deterministic framework.

Additionally, the discussion of tachyons invites comparisons with other speculative concepts in metaphysics, such as parallel universes and alternate timelines. If tachyons operate in a manner where information can flow fluidly across time and space, one might wonder if they necessitate the existence of a multiverse—a reality where multiple parallel dimensions coexist, each shaped by different histories and futures. The implications of such premises invite inquiries that reach beyond the confines of empirical science into speculative philosophical territories steeped in ethical and existential considerations.

Critics of tachyon theory often argue that without empirical evidence, such discussions remain firmly within the realm of metaphysical conjecture rather than scientific inquiry. The philosophical skepticism surrounding tachyons suggests that while it is crucial to remain open to imaginative possibilities, it is equally essential to ground our philosophies in observable phenomena. The tension between the desire to explore bold ideas and the necessity for empirical validation serves as a reminder that scientific advancement is as much a matter of evidence-based reasoning as it is of imaginative speculation.

Furthermore, the philosophical underpinnings of tachyon theory provoke reflections on human perception and understanding. If superluminal particles truly exist and challenge current paradigms, this not only broadens our scientific horizons but also reshapes our understanding of reality itself. The exploration of tachyons compels us to engage with fundamental questions, such as: What is time? What is the nature of reality? How do we perceive causation, and how might our understanding of self and existence shift if tachyons were shown to be a component of the universe?

These inquiries are not mere academic exercises; they resonate deeply with humanity's quest for meaning and understanding in the cosmos. In this pursuit, the philosophical critique of tachyons serves a transformative purpose, prompting us to cultivate an awareness of the limitations of our current frameworks while inviting us to explore broader existential questions that shape our understanding of the universe.

In conclusion, the philosophical counterarguments concerning tachyons challenge us to reevaluate our conceptions of time, causality, and existence. Addressing the metaphysical ramifications of these hypothetical particles promotes a dialogue that transcends scientific speculation, ultimately leading us to confront profound questions that weave together the narratives of science and philosophy. As our inquiry into the nature of reality continues, the interplay between tachyons and these existential reflections shall remain a vital aspect of our quest for knowledge—urging us to explore not just what exists, but what it means to exist within the vast cosmos we inhabit.

8.3. False Leads and Pseudoscience

In the realm of scientific inquiry, the pursuit of understanding tachyons—hypothetical particles theorized to travel faster than light —often unearths a contentious terrain rife with misconceptions and misinterpretations. Despite the fascination that tachyons evoke in popular science and science fiction alike, they have become embroiled in debates that straddle the boundaries of legitimate scientific investigation and pseudoscience. Here, we explore the implications of false leads surrounding tachyon research and the broader significance of maintaining a critical perspective within scientific discourse.

First, it is essential to address the landscape of misconceptions that often surround tachyon theory. The concept of tachyons, given their superluminal nature, invites sensationalist narratives that can blur the lines between rigorous scientific hypothesis and speculative fiction. Many enthusiasts assert that tachyons could enable instantaneous communication or even time travel, leading to misconceptions that these particles inherently defy all established physical laws. Such oversimplifications propagate an allure that is not rooted in scientific viability, diverting attention from the complexities inherent in serious scientific exploration.

A pivotal point to highlight is that the fascination with tachyons often fuels the emergence of pseudoscientific claims. As theories surrounding superluminal particles gain traction in popular media, various pseudoscientific movements latch onto the concept, discrediting genuine inquiries while offering sensationalized interpretations. This phenomenon can result in the proliferation of erroneous theories—asserting capabilities that tachyons do not possess—thereby obscuring the actual fundamentals of theoretical physics. The need for discernment between scientific fact and pseudoscience becomes paramount, as the latter can hinder progress by clouding discussions and drawing interest away from credible avenues of research.

The examination of false leads extends to the portrayal of tachyons in popular culture and media, often amplifying misconceptions while neglecting the rigor of scientific inquiry. The depiction of tachyons as magical solutions to the mysteries of time travel or instantaneous communication resonates with audiences; however, such portrayals tend to strip away the complexity and nuance integral to the pursuit of knowledge in physics. Media representations frequently prioritize entertainment value over scientific accuracy, leading to public understandings that may significantly deviate from the realities of particle physics.

Furthermore, the notion that tachyons could play a role in existing scientific frameworks often leads researchers into speculative traps. In recent discussions, some have attempted to connect tachyon dynamics with dark matter and dark energy, positing that these superluminal particles could provide answers to unresolved cosmological mysteries. While this ambition fosters critical inquiry, it can also veer into pseudoscientific territory when assertions lack empirical validation and credible theoretical backing. A balanced approach that prioritizes rigorous scientific methodology—coupled with healthy skepticism—remains vital to preventing the emergence of unfounded claims that may dilute the integrity of scientific discourse.

To navigate these complexities, scientists, educators, and communicators must work collaboratively to cultivate an informed public regarding tachyons and the broader implications of their study. Engaging in clear, accessible discussions about the limitations and challenges within tachyon research serves to demystify the narratives that surround these particles. By articulating the nuanced dialogues and diverse inquiries that characterize legitimate scientific exploration, we can underscore the importance of critical thinking and empirical evidence in fostering informed discussions.

In summary, the landscape of tachyon research is fraught with misconceptions and false leads that can obscure legitimate scientific inquiry and foster pseudoscientific narratives. To advance our understanding of tachyons and their implications, a commitment to rigorous methodology, healthy skepticism, and informed dialogue is imperative. As we strive to bridge the gap between theoretical exploration and empirical evidence, we reinforce the values of scientific inquiry, ensuring that genuine endeavors receive the attention and scrutiny they warrant within the broader context of knowledge. The journey of understanding tachyons epitomizes the ongoing tension between speculation and evidence—a tension that lies at the heart of the scientific quest to ascertain the mysteries of the universe.

8.4. Rational Deconstructions

In the exploration of tachyons, the hypothetical particles theorized to surpass the speed of light, a need arises to critically analyze and rationally deconstruct various concepts that have emerged within the scientific discourse. This scrutiny helps clarify the distinction between scientific hypotheses and speculative assertions that lack robust empirical support. Tachyons challenge our foundational understanding of speed, time, and causality, yet the debates surrounding them sometimes blur the lines between validated science and speculative fiction. Critiques of certain tachyon ideas can significantly enhance our comprehension of physical laws while reinforcing the necessity of a disciplined scientific inquiry.

One prominent challenge to tachyon theory is rooted in its conflict with established principles of relativity. Einstein's theories of special and general relativity provide a well-founded understanding of how mass, energy, and speed correlate with the very structure of spacetime. The very introduction of imaginary mass—an essential characteristic of tachyons—sparks concerns about coherence with the energy-momentum relations explicitly defined by these theories. Critics assert that not only do tachyons violate Einstein's universal speed limit, but they also potentially undermine the predictive power of relativity, leading to logical inconsistencies without adequate evidence or theoretical justification.

Moreover, the proposed ability of tachyons to facilitate retrocausality —where future states influence past events—brings significant philosophical implications. The linearity of time is a well-established concept in the framework of causality, and the idea that effects could precede their causes disrupts conventional causal chains. Supporters of tachyon theory may argue that this deviation opens new pathways of understanding temporal mechanics; however, skeptics contend that such propositions may lead to paradoxes reminiscent of classic time travel dilemmas, thereby vilifying the very framework that science seeks to maintain—one grounded in consistent, observable, and logical outcomes.

The empirical quest for tachyons faces the critical obstacle of direct detection. Despite the theoretical formulations available, experimental physics operates on the foundation of observable evidence. Critics point out that multiple proposed methodologies for discovering tachyons often lack the empirical grounding essential for acceptance within any scientific community. When researchers venture into the realms of high-energy particle collisions or cosmic ray observations while searching for superluminal signatures, it becomes imperative to measure results carefully and differentiate meaningful data from random noise or insignificant fluctuations.

Another area of skepticism arises concerning the speculative nature of research surrounding tachyons. The allure of instantaneous communication and fantastical applications can yield broad misconceptions leading researchers and the public alike into hyperbolic interpretations of potential findings. Taken out of context, these speculations can hinder the seriousness with which the scientific community approaches the hypotheses regarding tachyons, further complicating efforts to conduct foundational research. For scientists engaged in these inquiries, there rests a responsibility to maintain methodological rigor while communicating ideas accurately, fostering informed discussion while preventing hyperbolic claims detached from empirical realities.

Thus, engaging in rational deconstructions of tachyon-related concepts serves a dual purpose—providing clarity and shedding light on the nuances inherent in this arena of inquiry. This critical analysis invites us to maintain healthy skepticism, recognizing that rigorous scientific advancement often relies on patience and discerning scrutiny rather than jumping eagerly at the allure of revolutionary claims. By dissecting speculative assertions, scientists can better navigate the complexities surrounding tachyons, ensuring a methodical approach that aligns with established scientific principles.

In conclusion, the quest to comprehend tachyons is replete with philosophical implications, scientific challenges, and intriguing possibilities. Rational deconstructions within this field emphasize the importance of maintaining rigorous scientific standards while concurrently fostering a critical examination of speculative ideas. Although tachyons provoke spirited debate and intellectual curiosity, it is through disciplined inquiry and clear communication that the scientific community will continue to advance in its understanding of these enigmatic particles and their potential implications for the cosmos. As the conversations surrounding tachyons evolve, the interplay between skepticism and exploration drives us forward, challenging us to unfurl the tapestry of understanding within which these hypothetical particles might reside.

8.5. A Healthy Debate: Conclusion

Throughout the expansive examination of tachyons and the discussions surrounding their implications, we've traversed a rich landscape of scientific inquiry intertwining with philosophical reflections. In this concluding section, the focus is placed on the importance of skepticism in scientific advancement, particularly in relation to speculative theories such as those involving tachyons. Our journey through the folds of theoretical exploration, experimental challenges, philosophical debates, and scientific skepticism marks a critical phase in understanding the broader narrative of what tachyons represent within the scientific community.

Skepticism serves as a foundational pillar in the quest for knowledge, enabling researchers to drive inquiries with rigor and discipline. The pathway of scientific discovery has historically flourished through a culture that embraces critical examination of hypotheses, theories, and methodologies. When confronting ideas as audacious as faster-than-light travel via tachyons, skepticism compels scientists to maintain stringent standards for evidence, ensuring that assertions are robustly scrutinized before being integrated into established frameworks.

In the case of tachyons, their existence remains a subject of contention, fundamentally rooted in their challenge to our understanding of fundamental principles such as causality and the structure of spacetime. Without empirical evidence to substantiate their theoretical propositions, it is crucial to approach their study with caution and a commitment to rigorous validation. By adopting a skeptical stance, researchers ensure that the pursuit of knowledge adheres to the principles of the scientific method—acknowledging that speculation, while a driver of curiosity, cannot replace incontrovertible evidence.

Moreover, skepticism promotes healthy dialogue within the scientific community, encouraging scientists to engage with multiple perspectives and interpretations of phenomena. The debates surrounding tachyons exemplify how differing viewpoints can catalyze deeper understanding—pushing boundaries and expanding the frontiers of inquiry. Engaging with critics and addressing their concerns strengthens the validity of the research, leading to more comprehensive explorations and robust theories. Through this process, scientists refine their hypotheses, sometimes leading to unforeseen pathways that may amplify our comprehension of complex phenomena.

The dynamic interplay between skepticism and exploration also serves to delineate the boundaries between legitimate scientific inquiry and pseudoscience. As speculative ideas capture public imagination, it becomes imperative to differentiate between scientifically grounded discussions and sensationalized claims. By promoting skepticism, the scientific community can combat the allure of pseudoscientific narratives that often arise alongside fascinating theories like those concerning tachyons. This vigilance protects the integrity of the scientific discourse and promotes informed public understanding.

As we look forward to the prospect of future research into tachyons and their implications, a robust foundation of skepticism equips the scientific community to negotiate the challenges ahead. Whether through experimental pursuits in cosmic exploration, theoretical modeling, or interdisciplinary collaboration, skepticism will foster an environment where innovative ideas can flourish without veering into realms of unfounded speculation.

In summary, the exploration of tachyons serves as an exemplary case study in the critically intertwined relationship between skepticism and scientific advancement. This healthy debate nurtures inquiry, enabling researchers to navigate the complexities surrounding speculative theories while remaining firmly grounded in empirical evaluation. As we move forward, the emphasis on rigorous scrutiny will not only elevate discussions surrounding tachyons but will also enrich the broader narrative of scientific exploration—one that encourages curiosity while ensuring that the standards of evidence remain paramount in humanity's quest to unlock the mysteries of the universe. In doing so, we reaffirm our commitment to scientific discovery, eager to embrace future challenges with an open yet discerning mind.

9. Applications and Possibilities

9.1. Future Technologies Enabled by Tachyons

As we look to the horizon of scientific advancement, the prospect of tachyons embodies a tantalizing blend of theoretical exploration and practical innovation that has the potential to revolutionize technology and our understanding of the universe. Imagine a world in which the manipulation of tachyons could lead to breakthroughs across various fields, from energy production to transportation. While the notion of superluminal particles may sound like science fiction, their implications extend to realms of possibility where the fabric of reality can be reshaped by human ingenuity.

In the domain of energy, tachyons could provide novel methods for harnessing power. Given their hypothetical ability to transport energy instantaneously, the exploration of tachyon dynamics might inspire the development of new energy systems that leverage their unique properties. For instance, imagine power grids that rely on the transfer of energy via tachyonic channels, enabling instantaneous energy distribution across vast distances, eliminating lag time in energy flow, and potentially enhancing the efficiency of renewable energy sources. Such advancements could contribute to global energy sustainability, revolutionizing how we generate, transmit, and utilize power.

Transportation, too, may be transformed through tachyon research. The theoretical foundations suggest that if tachyons could be harnessed effectively, they might pave the way for entirely new forms of transit—craft that can traverse cosmic distances in the blink of an eye. Engineering marvels based on tachyonic principles could redefine space travel, allowing humans to journey to distant stars in a fraction of the time currently deemed possible. By reimagining propulsion systems and flight dynamics in light of tachyon behaviors, humanity could cultivate interstellar exploration as a viable reality, ushering in a new era of discovery.

Moreover, the influence of tachyon research extends into the realm of communications. Imagine instantaneous data transmission across the cosmos, where information can traverse vast distances without the constraints imposed by the speed of light. Tachyons offer the possibility of redefining communication networks to facilitate real-time interactions between disparate locations. Such capabilities could enable global networks that allow for seamless connectivity, fostering collaboration and information sharing that transcends traditional boundaries.

In the field of medicine and biological sciences, the inquiry into tachyonic interactions may potentially yield unprecedented advancements in health innovations. Researchers hypothesize that if tachyons can interact uniquely with biological systems, they might lead to breakthroughs in non-invasive diagnostics, such as imaging techniques or targeted therapies. The implications could revolutionize our approach to assessing and treating diseases, enhancing the quality of care and the effectiveness of medical interventions while minimizing side effects. Furthermore, understanding the peculiar behaviors of tachyons could invite novel approaches to biophysics, deepening our comprehension of life at the subatomic level.

The implications of tachyons stretch beyond purely technological advancements, inviting philosophical inquiry into their potential applications. Consider the impact of manipulating time—if tachyons indeed allow for superluminal interactions, then human application in time perception and time management may emerge. Philosophically, this invites profound considerations about daily life, free will, and even the nature of existence. The prospect of manipulating time could lead to changes in how we structure society, understand events, and engage with our individual experiences—creating a fundamentally different relationship with the flow of time.

In essence, the exploration of tachyons encapsulates a journey filled with sublime possibilities that may reshape our technological, philosophical, and societal landscapes. As scientific inquiry continues to probe the feasibility and ramifications of these hypothetical particles, we find ourselves at the nexus of imagination and practicality. The advancements expected in the fields enabled by tachyon study promise not just to expand the horizons of what is technically achievable but to enhance the human experience as we engage with the universe in ways previously thought to be the purview of myth and dreams.

As we embark on this speculative frontier, it is essential to maintain an informed sense of curiosity, grounded by disciplined methodology. Ongoing research into tachyons carries the potential to unlock new paradigms, pushing the boundaries of what can be realized from the theoretical into the tangible, serving as a testament to humanity's insatiable quest for knowledge and understanding. Ultimately, the future technologies enabled by tachyons symbolize the aspirations of a society willing to embrace the unknown, ever seeking to illuminate the mysteries woven into the fabric of existence.

9.2. Communications: Beyond Faster-Than-Light

In the realm of communication, tachyons—hypothetical particles theorized to exceed the speed of light—could redefine the conventional understanding of information transfer across the universe. Envision the implications of harnessing the dynamics of superluminal particles not only to accelerate the flow of information but also to fundamentally alter how signals traverse vast cosmic gulfs instantly. This exploration of tachyon-based communications invites speculation on the transformative potential of real-time data transfer that transcends the limitations imposed by present technologies.

Traditional communication methods rely on electromagnetic waves, which traverse space at finite speeds dictated by the speed of light. Even the most advanced communication technologies experience latencies and delays, particularly when signals are transmitted over great distances—factors that can hinder instantaneous interaction. Tachyonic communication, posited as a capability derived from harnessing superluminal properties, raises tantalizing questions about overcoming these constraints entirely. Imagine a communication network where signals conveyed through tachyon interactions could facilitate immediate responses between galaxies, allowing for seamless dialogue and collaboration on cosmic scales.

The implications of such groundbreaking communication systems extend into realms that bridge scientific practice with sociopolitical dimensions. From enhancing interstellar exchanges to fostering collaboration between distant spacefarers, the essence of human connection transcended by a network of instantaneous communication would fundamentally reshape not only societal structures but also the nature of collective experiences shared across civilizations. Moreover, this paradigm shift might cultivate an environment rife with opportunities for knowledge sharing, where insights from civilizations across the cosmos can enrich the collective understanding of existence itself.

Moreover, envision the implications on global networks on Earth if tachyonic communication were made feasible. The possibilities range from enhanced emergency response systems—where information relayed instantaneously could save lives—to global collaboration efforts tackling climate change, resource management, and technological innovations. The potential for a world interconnected by superluminal communication would foster a heightened awareness of our shared existence, transcending the geographical and cultural boundaries currently defining human interaction.

Furthermore, exploring tachyonic communication systems invites philosophical considerations regarding the nature of information itself. If the fundamental principles governing communication change, one might question if the essence of knowledge, understanding, and even emotional connections shifts in a tangible way. Could the manipulation of information transcended by tachyon dynamics engender new forms of relationships—new paradigms of interaction amongst individuals and societies?

Addressing the challenges associated with developing tachyonic communication technologies necessitates engaging interdisciplinary collaborations that fuse theoretical physics, engineering, and information technology. The exploration of tachyon dynamics in communication systems requires innovative thinking, leveraging advanced computational techniques, intrepid research, and robust theoretical models that correspond with the cutting-edge inquiries characterizing modern physics.

In approaching the task of realizing tachyon communications, it is integral to ground proposals in empirical science as we build theoretical frameworks for superluminal transmission systems. The speculation surrounding tachyonic communication—even if it remains unproven—invites researchers to engage with fundamental principles, analyze existing data, and develop mathematical models that encapsulate the unique properties of these elusive particles.

In conclusion, the potential for tachyons to redefine communication networks beckons exploration at the intersection of science, technology, and human connection. The vision of instantaneous information transfer shifts the landscape of human interaction, inspiring imaginative inquiries that extend beyond traditional boundaries. As researchers embark on this speculative frontier, they cultivate a fertile ground for innovation that could unlock novel frameworks for connection across the universe—illuminating the pathways by which humanity can engage with the cosmos and one another in ways previously deemed unimaginable. This journey into the future, driven by the potential of tachyon communications, embodies humanity's perpetual quest for knowledge, connection, and understanding amidst the vast tapestry of existence.

9.3. Tachyonic Influence on Medicine and Biological Science

In the grand landscape of science, tachyons are poised to offer innovative solutions and profound insights into the role of superluminal particles within medicine and biological sciences. As research on tachyons evolves, intriguing theories suggest that these hypothetical particles could not only expand our understanding of physical laws but also open pathways to groundbreaking advancements in health and medicine.

At the forefront of this exploration lies the possibility of employing tachyons as non-invasive diagnostic tools. Given their theorized interactions with electromagnetic fields, tachyons might possess unique properties that allow them to penetrate biological tissues without causing harm. This could revolutionize medical imaging techniques, providing enhanced imaging modalities that replace or complement traditional methods like X-rays, MRIs, and CT scans. Imagine a diagnostic technique where tachyonic particles align and resonate with molecular structures within the body, offering real-time imaging of internal processes with unprecedented clarity. This would not only reduce patient exposure to harmful radiation but also improve the accuracy and efficacy of diagnostics.

In tandem with imaging capabilities, the application of tachyon dynamics could facilitate targeted therapy strategies in which tachyons are deployed to interact specifically with diseased cells or tissues. By leveraging their hypothetical ability to traverse space and time instantaneously, medical practitioners could potentially use tachyons to deliver therapies directly to the target site, minimizing side effects and enhancing treatment efficacy. This could herald a new era in targeted cancer therapies, where tachyonic interactions amplify the delivery of chemotherapeutic agents to malignant cells, thereby reducing exposure to healthy tissues and enhancing overall patient outcomes.

Moreover, understanding the role of tachyons may lead to novel insights into the biological processes underpinning life itself. The hypothetical properties of these particles could allow researchers to investigate fundamental biological mechanisms, such as cellular communication and signaling pathways, through the lens of superluminal travel. This expanded perspective might unlock new approaches to understanding how biological systems operate at the quantum level, catalyzing innovations in fields such as genetics, bioinformatics, and systems biology. By exploring how tachyonic influences modulate cellular behavior or intercellular communications, scientists could develop therapies grounded in a profoundly nuanced understanding of life's mechanics.

The theoretical foundations also suggest that tachyons could impact broader applications in pharmaceuticals and drug design. If tachyon dynamics reveal novel interactions within cellular environments, pharmaceutical researchers might re-conceptualize the design and delivery of new drugs, improving therapeutic efficacy. For example, designing drugs that mimic tachyonic interactions could enhance the targeting of biochemical pathways altered in diseases.

Furthermore, the integration of tachyon theory into the biomedical field raises key ethical considerations and challenges. If we come to harness tachyon technology for medical advancements, questions inevitably arise concerning access, safety, and the implications of manipulating time and space within human bodies. Prompting discussions on best practices and regulatory frameworks will ensure that the exploration of tachyon applications maintains ethical standards while balancing innovation with patient safety.

As research efforts continue to unfold, it is essential for interdisciplinary collaboration to flourish among physicists, engineers, biologists, and ethicists. Fostering an environment where diverse expertise converges will lead to richer investigations into the potential of tachyons in medicine, engaging the scientific community in a collective effort to refine theories and explore tangible applications.

In summary, the exploration of tachyon influence on medicine and biological sciences paves the way for groundbreaking developments that may redefine healthcare. Through innovative applications in diagnostics, therapeutics, and cellular research, tachyons hold the potential to unlock extraordinary advancements in human health and understanding the nuances of life. As we embark on this exploratory journey into the possible applications of superluminal particles, we weave together the threads of scientific curiosity, innovation, and ethical responsibility—setting the stage for a transformative future in medicine driven by the quest for knowledge.

9.4. Theoretical Travel Engines Using Tachyons

The introduction of tachyons into theoretical physics not only beckons intriguing possibilities related to superluminal travel but also propels discussions about their application in creating advanced travel engines. Within this speculative framework, the capacity to harness tachyon dynamics could radically alter our approach to transportation, both on Earth and in space. The emerging narrative around tachyon-driven travel engines imagines frameworks that defy the traditional constraints imposed by known physics, offering exciting prospects for exploration and human connectivity.

Central to the concept of tachyon-based travel engines is the fundamental premise that these hypothetical particles could enable propulsion systems that circumvent conventional limitations. If tachyons were to exist, their purported capacity to exceed the speed of light opens the door to the notion of instantaneous travel across vast distances. A theoretical travel engine designed on these principles might harness tachyonic propulsion to facilitate journeys between celestial bodies in a fraction of the time required by current technologies. This leap in capability would resonate deeply with our aspirations for interstellar exploration, transforming what was once regarded as science fiction into a tangible possibility.

One potential design for a tachyon-based travel engine could involve a mechanism that generates a field of tachyons, effectively allowing a spacecraft to be enveloped in a bubble that propels it beyond the speed of light. This concept draws inspiration from existing ideas in theoretical physics, such as the Alcubierre "warp" drive—a theoretical model that allows for faster-than-light travel without violating relativity by bending spacetime itself. By integrating tachyons into such a framework, researchers could explore designs that dynamically manipulate spacetime, creating pathways that allow space vehicles to navigate the cosmos without the limitations imposed by light-speed constraints.

Moreover, engineering tachyonic systems might foster solutions to challenges currently encountered in space exploration, such as energy consumption, travel time, and life support during long-duration missions. Tachyon engines could effectively minimize fuel requirements and travel times while maintaining the structural integrity and safety of spacecraft. The implications of such advancements stretch beyond the technical, potentially reshaping our understanding of human presence in the cosmos and how we approach interstellar colonization.

However, the complexities inherent in the development of tachyon travel engines demand a careful balance between theoretical imagination and practical engineering. As researchers engage with the intricacies of tachyon theory, grounding our understanding in empirical science and rigorous experimentation remains crucial. Theoretical models must be continuously refined to account for the relationships between tachyons, energy systems, and the broader context of cosmic principles that govern our universe.

In evaluating these possibilities, it also becomes essential to engage with the philosophical implications of tachyon travel. How would instantaneous transportation reshape societal structures, cultural interactions, and our perception of time? The thought of immediate travel across the cosmos begs questions about identity, continuity, and relationships in a world where distance is rendered irrelevant.

Furthermore, the integration of tachyons within future travel technologies requires a robust ethical framework that navigates the social and environmental implications of space travel. As we envisage a future equipped with advanced tachyon engines, discussions surrounding access, safety, and the responsibilities associated with interstellar exploration take on heightened significance. These conversations will inevitably shape both policy and technology, ensuring that the journey toward harnessing tachyons aligns with humanity's broader aspirations for equity and stewardship.

In conclusion, the speculative exploration of theoretical travel engines utilizing tachyons pushes at the boundaries of scientific inquiry and human imagination. As researchers seek to visualize the mechanisms that could facilitate superluminal travel, they embark on quests that blend physics, engineering, and philosophical reflection into a cohesive narrative. Each conjecture surrounding tachyon-driven technologies influences the trajectory of future space exploration, shaping humanity's relationship with the cosmos and our understanding of existence itself. The path forward is one paved with potential and promise—inviting us to contemplate the limitless horizons of possibility that tachyons could unlock in our quest to traverse the vastness of time and space.

9.5. Time Manipulation and Human Application

In exploring the possibilities of time manipulation and human application through the lens of tachyon theory, we enter a fascinating interplay between science, philosophy, and practical implications that challenge our conventional understanding of time itself. As we investigate the hypothetical characteristics of tachyons—particles posited to travel faster than the speed of light—a plethora of questions emerges that probe not only the theoretical bounds of physics but also the potential impacts on human experience, societal constructs, and our very perception of existence.

Time, as understood in physics, has typically been perceived as a linear progression where the past informs the present, and the present shapes the future. Yet, the concept of tachyons disrupts this conventional flow by introducing scenarios wherein information, or influence, could traverse from the future to the past. This shift provokes profound philosophical questions about causality, free will, and the determination of fate. If tachyons allowed for retrocausality —where effects could precede their causes—how would we interpret our experiences and decisions? Would our perception of agency and accountability shift in a framework where the future could exert influence over the past? The implications spark rich dialogues about human responsibility in a universe that embraces non-linear temporal interactions.

As we contemplate practical applications of such theoretical constructs, the potential for time manipulation raises intriguing possibilities for enhancing human life. Consider the prospect of developing technologies that leverage the superluminal properties of tachyons. If communication through tachyons were feasible, real-time interactions across spatial and temporal barriers could redefine social dynamics, fostering instantaneous connectivity between individuals regardless of distance. Imagine holding a conversation with someone across the galaxy without the delays inherent in traditional communication methods—this reinforces the idea of a more interconnected experience of existence.

In a medical context, the application of tachyons could enable instantaneous diagnostics by allowing healthcare professionals to access a patient's historical medical data at superluminal speeds. This would facilitate timely interventions, potentially saving lives while enhancing the overall efficacy of healthcare practices. The promise of instantaneous information transfer opens a myriad of possibilities, from improving emergency response systems to accelerating drug development processes by providing instant feedback on emerging data.

However, at the heart of all these advancements also lies the ethical consideration of manipulating time. As we contemplate the ability to influence temporal mechanics through tachyons, we must grapple with the consequences that non-linear interactions could impose on human society. Would this technology create inequalities, where only certain individuals or corporations could access the benefits of time manipulation? Discussions surrounding equitable access to such transformative technologies must become integral to any exploration of tachyon applications in human life.

Beyond practical implications, the philosophical dimensions of time manipulation also invite us to reconsider intrinsic human experiences. Our cultural narratives—stories, myths, and traditions—are often interwoven with the linear understanding of time. By introducing tachyons into our consciousness, we may begin to question our relationship with time itself: how we experience nostalgia, anticipation, and the unfolding of life's events. If time is fluid and influenced by superluminal particles, then perhaps our emotional understanding of experiences could evolve, prompting us to cultivate new ways of relating to our past and envisioning our future.

Thus, the exploration of tachyonic time manipulation invites us to embody both curiosity and caution. The concept of time, now overlapping with principles that remain largely theoretical, challenges us to engage with the ethical, philosophical, and practical implications that arise from this inquiry. As we conceive potential applications, we must do so with mindfulness of the broader human experience, ensuring that innovations are pursued alongside a commitment to equity, responsibility, and the pursuit of wisdom derived from our understanding of time.

In conclusion, the intersection of tachyons and time manipulation opens up a tantalizing domain of exploration that empowers us to rethink how we perceive and interact with time. By addressing the challenges and possibilities inherent in this pursuit, we embrace a journey that not only pushes the frontiers of science but enriches our understanding of existence itself. As we stand at the precipice of these speculative inquiries, we are reminded that time, as both a scientific and human construct, is a rich tapestry—awaiting our continued engagement as we seek to uncover the profound mysteries woven into its fabric.

10. When Science Meets Fiction: Tachyons in Media

10.1. The Birth of a Sci-Fi Concept

The exploration of tachyons, the hypothetical particles theorized to traverse faster than light, represents a captivating junction of scientific inquiry and imaginative speculation. Often characterized by their peculiar properties, tachyons have not only sparked debates in the realms of physics but have also made significant inroads into the sphere of popular culture, particularly within science fiction. The concept of tachyons serves as a template for exploring complex themes surrounding time, speed, and the nature of reality, placing them at the forefront of imaginative narratives that bridge the gap between theoretical science and creative storytelling.

The engagement of tachyons with public consciousness is largely rooted in their portrayal within science fiction. Authors and filmmakers have seized upon the idea of these superluminal particles to explore the fascinating implications of time travel, instantaneous communication, and the nature of causality. The origins of tachyons in popular culture trace back to early theoretical discussions in physics, where the notion of faster-than-light travel was emerging in tandem with the development of concepts in relativity. Writers began to weave scientific theories into their narratives, depicting tachyons as fantastical tools to manipulate time and space, capturing imaginations and laying the groundwork for thrilling plots that questioned the very fabric of existence.

From classics like Philip K. Dick's works to contemporary projects, tachyons have often been utilized as devices that enable characters to embark on extraordinary journeys through time and alternate realities. These literary explorations invite readers to contemplate profound questions about destiny, energetic connections that cross temporal boundaries, and the interconnectedness of even the most distant events. By employing tachyons as plot devices, authors delve into themes of free will and determinism—inviting audiences to ponder the profound ethical implications of time manipulation and the responsibilities that accompany such powers.

In the realm of film, tachyons have been referenced as pivotal elements in narratives that navigate complex temporal mechanics. Movies like "Star Trek" and various adaptations of time-focused science fiction frequently evoke the concept of tachyons to justify rapid travel across vast distances or the retransmission of messages across time. These representations encapsulate the allure of tachyons as agents capable of reshaping character destinies and altering the course of historical events. Filmic interpretations often omit the intricacies of tachyon physics, instead opting for a more stylized portrayal that trades scientific accuracy for dramatic effect, enhancing viewers' attempts to grasp the significance of time travel and its consequences.

Television also showcases a rich tapestry of representations of tachyons. Popular series like "Doctor Who" and "Fringe" deftly intertwine scientific speculation with imaginative narratives, utilizing tachyons as mechanisms to propel their storylines through complex plots involving alternate realities, paradoxes, and the true nature of existence. These portrayals not only entertain but also provoke contemplation around scientific concepts, often igniting curiosity among viewers regarding the actual physics behind tachyons and challenging them to distinguish between fact and fiction.

The influence of tachyons has permeated beyond traditional media into broader pop culture, encapsulating a growing fascination with the idea of breaking temporal boundaries. Products—ranging from video games to graphic novels—have showcased tachyons and superluminal travel, reflecting society's enduring interest in the possibilities of transcending limitations imposed by time and space. This infusion of scientific concepts into everyday entertainment underscores a societal enthusiasm for exploration, particularly as it relates to the mysteries of the universe.

Nevertheless, it is vital to draw distinctions between the fictional narratives surrounding tachyons and the realities of scientific investigation. The exhilarating depiction of tachyon-driven technologies in media often glosses over the complexities and challenges inherent in objectively studying superluminal particles. This divergence raises essential conversations about the responsibilities of creators in popularizing scientific concepts while maintaining fidelity to the underlying principles of science. Moreover, it invites audiences to engage critically with representations, discerning between entertainment and authentic scientific inquiry.

In summary, the intersection of tachyons and popular culture reveals a profound interplay between scientific speculation and imaginative storytelling. From literature to film and television, the portrayal of these hypothetical particles fosters discussions surrounding time, fate, and the nature of reality, capturing the public's imagination while delving into the philosophical questions posed by their existence. As we continue to explore the conceptual landscape surrounding tachyons, we are reminded of our capacity to merge scientific inquiry with creativity, offering us new pathways for understanding time travel, the cosmos, and our place within it.

10.2. Film and Literature Interpretations

The intersection of film and literature with the concept of tachyons represents a compelling exploration at the confluence of science and imagination. This subchapter delves deeply into how tachyon science has been interpreted, depicted, and utilized within various creative forms of media, reflecting society's fascination with the possibilities beyond our current scientific understanding.

In numerous works of science fiction literature, tachyons serve as a powerful narrative device for exploring themes of time travel, interstellar communication, and the nature of reality itself. Authors often capitalize on the allure of superluminal speeds, positioning tachyons as either the means to manipulate time or as the very fabric through which time itself can be understood. This literary treatment often draws on the rigorous principles of physics, albeit with creative license to expand the boundaries of plausible scientific inquiry into imaginative realms. Classic works, including those by renowned authors like Isaac Asimov and Arthur C. Clarke, frequently reference tachyons as a technological cornerstone, incorporating theoretical discussions on the relationships between space, time, and causality into engaging narratives that captivate audiences.

Films also embrace the concept of tachyons, though with varying degrees of fidelity to scientific principles. In cinematic portrayals, such as in the "Star Trek" franchise, tachyons are utilized to explain faster-than-light travel and instantaneous communication across vast distances. These films often mix scientific explanation with engaging storytelling, capturing the audience's imagination while offering tantalizing glimpses into a visceral future of exploration. However, these depictions may omit the complexities of hypothetical particle dynamics, prioritizing entertainment value over stringent adherence to scientific accuracy. Nevertheless, the influence of such portrayals on public consciousness fosters a broader interest in the underlying principles of physics and the speculative nature of tachyons.

Television series have similarly harnessed the concept of tachyons for dramatic effect, with shows like "Fringe" delving into alternate realities and complex scientific premises that often utilize tachyonic theories to drive their storylines. These narratives frequently engage with philosophical questions surrounding time travel, causality, and the nature of existence, inviting viewers to ponder the implications of technology that could manipulate time itself. By weaving tachyons into their plots, writers stimulate discussions that extend beyond the screen—capturing the curiosity of audiences eager to explore the possibilities of superluminal travel in both speculative fiction and real scientific discourse.

In exploring the influence of tachyons on pop culture, it becomes apparent that the concept has permeated various creative works beyond traditional literature and cinema. Video games, graphic novels, and comic books also feature tachyons or superluminal elements, often depicting technology that challenges the constraints of time and space. These depictions contribute to the broader narrative about humanity's relationship with the universe, as they invite players and readers to engage with themes reminiscent of both adventure and profound exploration.

However, amidst these artistic representations, it is crucial to differentiate between science fiction and genuine scientific potential. While tachyons captivate the imagination and encourage exploration of speculative ideas, critics warn against conflating entertainment with empirical science. The goals of scientific inquiry revolve around obtaining evidence and rigorous testing of ideas, whereas narratives often forge ahead with bold assertions that may lack empirical substantiation. This dichotomy invites audiences to engage critically, assessing the veracity of scientific claims while enjoying the creative interpretations of tachyon science in popular media.

As we examine the portrayals of tachyons across various media, we gain insight into the cultural impact of scientific concepts, highlighting how speculative ideas can shape public interest and dialogue in scientific exploration. This dialogue often transcends entertainment, paving the way for broader discussions about the implications of tachyons and the potential future of science itself. As we look to the future, it becomes clear that the relationship between tachyons as a scientific concept and their representation in films, literature, and television serves as a recurrent reminder of the capacity of human imagination to illuminate the potential that lies within the universe, while also challenging us to pursue a deeper understanding of the very nature of reality.

In conclusion, the interpretations of tachyons in film and literature underscore a rich interplay between scientific inquiry and creative expression that captures the imagination while prompting critical dialogues about existence, time, and the potential bound in the fabric of the cosmos. As we welcome an era where technology continues to evolve, the stories built around the concept of tachyons will likely inspire future generations to explore the depths of both science and imagination.

10.3. Television's Treatment of Tachyons

Television has long served as a fertile ground for exploring complex scientific concepts, distilling them into engaging narratives that captivate audiences while sparking their curiosity. Tachyons, the hypothetical particles theorized to travel faster than light, have found their way into various TV series, often serving as a plot mechanism to delve into themes surrounding time travel, alternate realities, and instantaneous communication. The treatment of tachyons in television showcases the delicate interplay between speculative fiction and scientific inquiry, as writers weave these concepts into compelling stories that resonate with both science enthusiasts and the general public alike.

In many popular science fiction series, tachyons are portrayed as pivotal elements facilitating advanced technology. For instance, in "Star Trek," tachyons are frequently referenced as components that enable spacecraft to travel at superluminal speeds, forming the basis for warp drive technology. This portrayal not only captivates the audience with the notion of interstellar travel but also introduces discussions about the feasible applications of tachyon theory within the context of human exploration of the cosmos. The series exploits the excitement surrounding tachyons, suggesting that the boundaries of current travel capabilities can be transcended through such innovations—a theme that resonates deeply within the overarching narrative of the franchise.

Other series, such as "Fringe," leverage tachions to explore the complexities of alternate realities and time manipulation. The show presents a world where the consequences of exploring tachyonic interactions lead to profound ramifications for characters caught in the web of time. By capturing scenarios where individuals may influence events across timelines, the series promotes contemplation about the nature of causation and human agency, echoing seminal philosophical debates around the implications of altering past experiences.

As audiences engage with these representations of tachyons, the portrayal often sparks deeper discussions about the nature of reality and the philosophical underpinnings of time. Tachyons challenge the audience to think critically about their relationship with time and existence, inviting them to ponder questions regarding free will, determinism, and the potential for multiple timelines—themes that resonate throughout science fiction. In this regard, television not only entertains but also serves as a medium for encouraging intellectual curiosity about scientific concepts.

However, while entertaining narratives unfold that incorporate tachyons, it remains essential to navigate the line between science fiction and reality. Although the concepts depicted in shows inspire imagination, they often skirt the edges of rigorous scientific under-standing. In particular, the simplifications made in the narrative often turn complex theoretical physics into digestible content—this can occasionally lead the audience to develop misconceptions about the scientific principles behind the portrayal. Nonetheless, this gap between fiction and reality provides an opportunity for science com-municators, educators, and enthusiasts to engage in discussions about what tachyons truly represent in modern physics.

Moreover, the treatment of tachyons in television series can influence public perception of scientific research, shaping how society views and understands cutting-edge scientific inquiries. As viewers become intrigued by the fantastical possibilities surrounding tachyons, they may also develop an increased interest in the actual science that explores these ideas. This engagement can cultivate a broader appre-ciation for scientific endeavors, prompting public support for research initiatives and education around particle physics and related fields.

In summary, television's treatment of tachyons reveals the dynamic interplay between speculative fiction and scientific inquiry, crafting compelling narratives that invite audiences to examine complex themes surrounding time, speed, and existence. Through the por-trayal of tachyons, series like "Star Trek" and "Fringe" foster curiosity while prompting critical discussions about the nature of reality. While these representations transport audiences to worlds shaped by imaginations, they simultaneously ignite interest in the actual science behind tachyons, reminding us of science fiction's role in inspiring future generations to explore the frontiers of knowledge. As we look ahead, the fusion of scientific inquiry and storytelling remains a potent tool to engage, educate, and inspire curiosity in a world full of possibilities.

10.4. Influence on Pop Culture

The influence of tachyons extends far beyond the confines of theoretical physics, permeating pop culture and inspiring a myriad of creative works across various mediums. This phenomenon reflects humanity's enduring fascination with concepts that challenge our fundamental understanding of reality, particularly those that engage with the ideas of time travel, instantaneous communication, and the very nature of existence. Tachyons serve as a gateway into speculative realms, fascinating both creators and audiences alike, igniting imagination and inquiry into the possibilities that lie at the fringes of science.

In literature, tachyons have become a staple trope in science fiction narratives. Authors frequently embed these hypothetical particles within their plots, utilizing them as vehicles for exploring complex themes. Works by renowned writers such as Philip K. Dick and Isaac Asimov integrate tachyon dynamics to engage with ideas of alternate realities, causality, and the implications of time manipulation. These literary explorations create rich narratives that invite readers to ponder profound questions about the nature of time, the paradoxes associated with time travel, and the interconnectedness of events.

Television series also embrace tachyons, weaving them into storylines that captivate viewers with thrilling explorations of superluminal travel and its implications. Shows like "Star Trek" and "Fringe" employ tachyons as plot devices, highlighting their potential for interstellar communication, warp-speed travel, and alternate timelines. These series not only entertain but encourage viewers to engage with scientific concepts, provoking inquiry into the feasibility of such technologies. In presenting tachyons as integral components of complex plots, producers inspire audiences to contemplate the boundaries of reality shaped by theoretical science.

The influence of tachyons has furthermore found its way into film, with notable representations showcasing their potential to facilitate rapid travel across vast distances. Movies often leverage tachyons to explain advanced technology that allows characters to traverse time and space, thus enriching the narrative while also provoking thoughtful discussions about the ethics and mechanics of time travel. The dramatization of tachyons in these films, while sometimes sacrificing scientific accuracy for storytelling, undeniably captures public interest, fostering curiosity about the actual science behind such phenomena.

Beyond traditional media, tachyons have permeated contemporary culture, including graphic novels, video games, and other entertainment platforms. These creative endeavors utilize tachyons and the notion of superluminal speed to craft immersive experiences where players and readers can manipulate time and manipulate reality. The infusion of scientific concepts into gaming and storytelling helps demystify complex theories, making them accessible and engaging for a broader audience. This interplay between science and creativity has empowered creators to draw upon tachyons as symbols of possibility, reflecting the human desire to stretch the boundaries of what is conceivable.

However, the allure of tachyons as a pop culture phenomenon also underscores the necessity of discernment between science fiction and scientifically grounded inquiry. While the creative interpretations of tachyons can inspire genuine enthusiasm for physics, it is crucial to engage critically with these representations. Education and public discourse must strive to distinguish speculative fiction from the rigorous validation demanded by scientific inquiry, ensuring that while interest in tachyons flourishes, it remains tethered to reality.

In conclusion, the influence of tachyons on pop culture exemplifies the intricate dialogue between scientific exploration and creative expression. As literature, television, and film leverage tachyon dynamics to explore complex themes of time and existence, they transform complex ideas into narratives that capture the imagination. This fusion of science and art serves not only as entertainment but also as an opportunity to foster curiosity about the mysteries of the universe. As we continue to navigate the landscapes shaped by tachyons and engage with their implications, we celebrate the power of creativity as a beacon guiding exploration into the uncharted realms of knowledge at the intersection of science and imagination.

10.5. Sci-Fi Versus Reality

In exploring the differences between science fiction and the scientific realities surrounding tachyons, we embark on a journey that illuminates both the allure and the challenges presented by these hypothetical particles. The fascination with tachyons often manifests in imaginative portrayals in literature, film, and television, where they serve as powerful narrative devices that facilitate extraordinary abilities such as time travel, instantaneous communication, and interstellar exploration. However, while these portrayals capture the public's imagination, they can sometimes obscure the intricacies and uncertainties of the genuine scientific inquiries surrounding tachyon research.

In science fiction, tachyons are frequently depicted as the means by which characters can manipulate the fabric of time and space, granting them abilities that transcend human limitations. Sci-fi narratives often take creative liberties to enhance plotlines, leading to engaging yet unrealistic portrayals of tachyon dynamics. For instance, in popular franchises like "Star Trek" or literary works by esteemed authors, tachyons are presented as integral components of fantastical technologies, allowing for warp drives or instantaneous data transmission across great distances. These narratives, while entertaining and thought-provoking, often gloss over the underlying physical theories and empirical challenges involved in grounding such ideas in reality.

Conversely, the scientific exploration of tachyons is steeped in rigorous theoretical inquiry, where researchers grapple with a host of complexities and limitations that have yet to be overcome. The existence of tachyons remains purely hypothetical, based on speculative interpretations of relativistic physics. Despite the provocative implications of superluminal particles, empirical evidence supporting their existence is markedly absent, and their study remains confined to the realms of theoretical physics and mathematical modeling. Scientists continue to navigate a landscape filled with skepticism, highlighting the challenges of demonstrating tachyon dynamics in laboratory experiments, decoding the implications for causality, and integrating such concepts into the broader framework of modern physics.

This dichotomy between science fiction and reality underscores key philosophical implications for our understanding of time, space, and existence. While fiction borrows from scientific principles to construct captivating narratives, it is imperative to maintain a distinction between artistic interpretation and scientific validation. As public intrigue in tachyons grows in tandem with their portrayal in popular media, the responsibility falls on researchers and communicators alike to provide clarity—that is, to explore the speculative nature of tachyon theories while anchoring discussions in empirical inquiry and established scientific principles.

Looking ahead, the conversation surrounding tachyons holds profound potential for shaping future scientific investigations. Upcoming research paths aim to explore the limits of our current understanding while encouraging dialogues about revolutionary concepts that could redefine our approach to time and causality. International collaborations among scientists are poised to facilitate the convergence of diverse perspectives and methodologies, generating holistic inquiries into the complexities of tachyon dynamics.

As we reflect on the prospects for tachyon research, we recognize the essential role it plays in fostering new paradigms within the scientific community—inviting both skepticism and curiosity as we seek to disentangle speculative fiction from the foundations of empirical science. The ongoing engagement with tachyon-related research challenges the boundaries of established knowledge, compelling us to expand our comprehension of the universe's intricacies while remaining vigilant about the differences between fictional narratives and scientific realities.

In conclusion, as we navigate the intersection between tachyons' representation in pop culture and the unfolding exploration of their scientific possibilities, it becomes imperative to foster an environment of informed inquiry. The narrative of tachyons serves as both inspiration and caution—a reflection of humanity's ever-curious spirit while anchoring our engagements in the empirical rigor that characterizes the scientific process. As we look to the future, the interface between scientific inquiry and imaginative exploration surrounding tachyons assures us that both realms are indelibly linked, shaping not only our understanding of the universe but also the questions that propel us into uncharted territories of knowledge and possibility.

11. Looking to the Future: Prospects for Tachyon Research

11.1. The Role of Tachyons in Future Science

The hypothesis of tachyons presents a unique and fascinating intersection where speculative science meets the aspirations of future scientific exploration. As researchers delve deeper into the complexities of these superluminal particles, it becomes evident that understanding tachyons may yield significant insights about the universe and help redefine our grasp of physics as we know it. The prospects for tachyon research span various fields, inviting innovative approaches to long-standing questions about the nature of time and space.

One promising area of inquiry involves probing into alternative framework theories within physics that could accommodate the existence of tachyons. Theoretical physicists actively engage in refining models that incorporate superluminal particles into contemporary quantum field theories or string theory, suggesting that these theories may not only support tachyonic phenomena but also contribute to our understanding of fundamental forces. Exploring the implications of tachyons within these frameworks may invite researchers to rethink existing paradigms of particle behavior and uncover connections previously overlooked.

Furthermore, advancements in experimental techniques present an exciting avenue for future tachyon research. Technological innovations in particle acceleration, detection methods, and data analysis provide opportunities to explore tachyon dynamics in greater depth. High-energy particle colliders, such as the Large Hadron Collider and the proposed Future Circular Collider, could facilitate targeted experiments geared towards identifying any tachyon-like signatures amidst the data generated in particle collisions. As equipment becomes more sensitive, the ability to discern unexpected signals could lead to revolutionary discoveries that naturally extend our understanding of the universe.

The cognitive leap that tachyons represent also extends to practical applications, sparking discussions around the potential for transformative technologies influenced by their hypothetical properties. For instance, should researchers successfully demonstrate the principles governing tachyon dynamics, avenues for instantaneous communication or innovative propulsion systems could emerge. Such breakthroughs might not only enhance space exploration but also revolutionize how we connect globally and interact with the cosmos. The excitement surrounding these possibilities fuels a desire for rigorous scientific inquiry aimed at translating theoretical insights into practical benefits.

Indeed, the culture of collaborative research plays a vital role in the future of tachyon science. Globalization has ushered in a new era of scientific collaboration where interdisciplinary teams from various countries and cultures converge to tackle complex challenges. The complexity of tachyon research necessitates such collaboration, as merging insights from theoretical physicists, experimental scientists, and engineers is paramount to advancing our understanding. By pooling resources and expertise, the scientific community can leverage a broader base of knowledge, enabling us to address the multifaceted questions and implications that arise within tachyon inquiry.

The training of the next generation of scientists, inspired by the promise inherent in tachyon exploration, will be foundational to the future landscape of physics. Educational frameworks that encourage curiosity-driven inquiry and empower students to engage with complex ideas promote an environment ripe for innovation. Universities and research institutions should foster programs that expose emerging scientists to both the theoretical and experimental dimensions surrounding tachyons and emerging interdisciplinary fields. This educational approach not only broadens the scientific workforce but also invigorates the quest for knowledge grounded in inspiration, creativity, and curiosity.

As we look to the future, the prospects for tachyon research offer a compelling testament to humanity's quest to understand the universe, replete with challenges and opportunities that can redefine the trajectory of scientific inquiry. Tachyons embody the intersections of imagination and rigorous investigation, driving us to question, explore, and expand the frontiers of what we know. In doing so, we reaffirm our commitment to unveiling the intricacies of existence and embracing the unknown as we continue our pursuit of knowledge in this vast cosmos. Through sustained inquiry and collaborative efforts across generations, tachyons might one day reveal the wonders of the universe yet to be uncovered, inspiring future discoveries that illuminate both science and the human experience in profound ways.

11.2. Global Tachyon Collaboration

The field of tachyon research, while largely theoretical, has prompted a growing international dialogue among scientists who are committed to exploring the possibilities these hypothetical particles present. The collaborative nature of this inquiry is not just beneficial but essential, fostering an environment where diverse perspectives converge to tackle complex questions. In this context, global tachyon collaboration has emerged as a critical driver of innovation and scientific progress, underlining the interconnectedness of the scientific community as it ventures into speculative terrain.

At the heart of global collaboration in tachyon research lies the shared goal of deepening our understanding of the fundamental laws of physics. Physicists around the world recognize that the investigation into tachyons encompasses a convergence of disciplines, including theoretical physics, quantum mechanics, astrophysics, and particle physics. This multidisciplinary approach allows researchers to borrow methodologies and insights from various fields, enriching the discourse and pushing the boundaries of knowledge. The pooling of resources, expertise, and data from multiple institutions enhances the rigor of proposed theories and experimental designs, ultimately honing the precision and scope of investigations.

One historic example of this collaborative spirit can be seen in international scientific projects like the Large Hadron Collider (LHC), where researchers from various countries come together to explore fundamental particles and their interactions. Within such collaborative frameworks, the potential for tachyon research becomes more accessible as theoretical models are scrutinized, experimental proposals refined, and findings shared across borders. When teams of scientists unite, they can work together to devise experimental strategies that could detect tachyons or uncover quanta indicative of superluminal behavior, transcending the limitations that individual efforts often encounter.

Moreover, emerging technologies, including artificial intelligence and machine learning, can be harnessed to facilitate global collaboration. Advanced data analysis techniques can sift through the vast datasets generated by high-energy experiments to discern patterns that suggest tachyonic behavior. As research teams increasingly adopt these innovative technologies, collaboration expands through collective data sharing and interpretations. This fusion of science and technology allows for a more dynamic exploration of tachyons, signaling the potential for breakthroughs that could reshape our understanding of particles and forces at large.

However, global tachyon collaboration extends beyond theoretical and experimental efforts; it encompasses the necessity to engage the public. Effective communication strategies will play an essential role in garnering interest and support for tachyon research on an international scale. By popularizing the science behind tachyons through accessible outreach initiatives—such as public lectures, educational content, and social media engagement—scientists can inspire curiosity and enthusiasm among diverse audiences. This public interest can catalyze funding opportunities, support educational initiatives, and attract a new generation of scientists eager to engage with the challenges and possibilities associated with tachyon investigations.

Furthermore, fostering a global community that emphasizes the ethical implications of tachyon research is crucial. The potential for tachyons to revolutionize technology and our understanding of reality calls for ongoing discussions surrounding the moral dimensions of their application. Open dialogues that span international borders will ensure that a diverse range of perspectives is incorporated into decision-making processes, particularly as the implications of tachyon technology extend into communication, transportation, and healthcare.

As we stand at the threshold of advancing tachyon science, global collaboration serves as the catalyst that allows us to confront this rich territory of inquiry with courage and determination. With every shared discovery, experimental effort, or theoretical insight, the pursuit of understanding tachyons reflects humanity's unyielding ambition to penetrate the mysteries of existence—and ultimately, re-define our understanding of time, space, and the interconnectedness of all knowledge.

In summary, global tachyon collaboration is vital to advancing the field of tachyon research. It embodies the spirit of shared inquiry, en-abling diverse and multidisciplinary contributions that enhance the-oretical and experimental investigations. This collaborative approach not only fosters scientific innovation but also elevates public engage-ment, ethical considerations, and educational initiatives—ensuring that the journey of exploration into tachyon science is both inclusive and impactful. As researchers embark on this journey, the profound implications of their work ripple across borders, contributing to a deeper understanding of the universe that awaits discovery.

11.3. Potential Game-Changers on the Horizon

As we peer into the future of tachyon research, one cannot help but recognize the potential game-changers that lie on the horizon. The exploration of tachyons—hypothetical particles theorized to travel faster than light—could unravel long-held understandings and ignite a new era of scientific innovation. In contemplating the possibilities that tachyons may offer, we must consider various dimensions in which their principles could lead to profound advancements in tech-nology and science.

One domain where the implications of tachyons are particularly compelling is in the realm of communication technologies. The notion of instantaneous information transfer via tachyonic signals is exhilarating and transformative. If researchers can develop a practical methodology for harnessing tachyon dynamics, we could witness technological advancements that allow information to be transmitted across vast cosmic distances without the time delays inherent in electromagnetic communication. This could redefine how societies interact, enabling real-time communication with deep-space missions or instantaneous exchanges of data across global networks. Such advancements might foster unprecedented collaboration in science, diplomacy, and trade on an interstellar scale.

Moreover, the prospect of using tachyons for energy transmission is equally enticing. With their theorized potential for superluminal travel, tachyons could facilitate processes that allow for instantaneous energy distribution, reducing loss encountered in traditional transmission methods. This capability might lead to the development of energy grids that operate with unparalleled efficiency, providing a sustainable solution to the global energy crisis. Furthermore, exploring tachyon dynamics could yield new energy-generation techniques, enhancing our approach to harnessing and storing renewable resources.

In addition to energy and communication, tachyon research could hold transformational implications for space exploration itself. The development of propulsion systems that employ tachyon dynamics could revolutionize how we navigate the cosmos. Spacecraft powered by tachyonic technology may traverse vast distances, reaching distant planets and star systems in a fraction of the time required by conventional technology. This evokes the dream of interstellar travel, expanding humanity's reach into the universe and potentially opening doors for colonization and resource acquisition on extraterrestrial worlds.

The implications of tachyons are not limited solely to scientific advancements. They resonate deeply with philosophical inquiries that challenge our understanding of time, existence, and the interconnectedness of all things. If tachyons can enable retrocausality

—where effects precede their causes—they may prompt a reevaluation of concepts like free will, determinism, and the nature of reality. In this context, the exploration of tachyons may catalyze a philosophical renaissance, urging humanity to reframe its relationship with time and existence itself.

As we anticipate these potential game-changers, we must also consider the importance of nurturing the next generation of scientists inspired to enter fields catalyzed by tachyon investigation. Educational initiatives that emphasize curiosity-driven inquiry, interdisciplinary collaboration, and engagement with complex ideas will be critical in shaping the future landscape of tachyon research. Curricula that foster foundational knowledge in theoretical and experimental physics —combined with exposure to emerging technologies and ethical considerations—will prepare young scientists to explore the uncharted territories of tachyon dynamics.

Encouraging mentorship and outreach programs can bridge the gap between established scientists and budding researchers, inviting diverse voices into the discourse surrounding tachyons. By creating opportunities for students to engage with the scientific community, we cultivate a workforce that can push the boundaries of knowledge and rethink paradigms that govern our understanding of the universe.

In summary, the potential game-changers on the horizon regarding tachyon research extend far beyond theoretical exploration. From revolutionizing communication and energy distribution to redefining humanity's relationship with time and existence, the implications are profound. By inspiring a new generation of scientists to engage deeply with these possibilities, we pave the way for transformative advancements that await as we venture into the unknown. The quest for knowledge surrounding tachyons not only illustrates the power of scientific inquiry but also reflects the spirit of exploration that resides at the core of humanity's quest to understand itself and the universe in which it exists. As we stand on this precipice, the horizon gleams with promise, beckoning eager minds to explore the tantalizing possibilities that tachyons may unveil.

11.4. New Paradigms in Physics

As we stand on the forefront of theoretical exploration in physics, the prospect of tachyons introduces the opportunity for new paradigms that could fundamentally reshape our understanding of scientific principles and the universe itself. Tachyons—hypothetical particles proposed to travel faster than light—have the potential to bridge gaps in existing theories and challenge long-held beliefs about the nature of reality. Their theoretical properties may not only energize discussions surrounding time travel and instantaneous communication but also provoke a reevaluation of foundational concepts in physics, including causality, space, and time.

One of the most significant areas where tachyons could lead to new paradigms is in the understanding of time. Traditionally, physics has adhered to a linear conception of time, wherein causes precede effects. However, if tachyons exist and can interact in ways that allow for retrocausal influences, it would force physicists to confront the limitations of classical thinking. The incorporation of tachyons into our models of time may lead to the development of a non-linear framework where events can be influenced by future conditions, fundamentally altering our grasp of temporal mechanics. This shift could yield revolutionary insights into the interconnectedness of past, present, and future, redefining how we understand causality in both everyday life and cosmic phenomena.

Additionally, the study of tachyons may prompt a reconfiguration of concepts surrounding speed and mass. The postulation of particles with imaginary mass challenges the very idea of what mass is and how it behaves at relativistic speeds. This could lead scientists to explore realms of particle dynamics that have remained uncharted, fostering the development of new theoretical frameworks that align more closely with quantum mechanics. As physicists investigate the implications of tachyon dynamics, they may uncover deeper insights into existing particle theories, potentially leading to a more unified understanding of forces and interactions across the universe.

Furthermore, the exploration of tachyons may yield contributions to the fields of cosmology and astrophysics. As researchers study the implications of superluminal particles, they can assess their potential impacts on cosmic phenomena, including the accelerating expansion of the universe and the elusive properties of dark matter and dark energy. Incorporating tachyons into cosmological models could challenge the conventional narratives surrounding these enigmatic forces, inspiring new research directions that may reshape our understanding of the universe's structure and evolution.

In essence, tachyons invite a rethinking of our scientific methodologies, challenging researchers to reconsider established principles while exploring speculative ideas. The pursuit of understanding tachyon dynamics invites environments for interdisciplinary collaboration, uniting physicists with engineers, mathematicians, and philosophers in the quest for knowledge. This collaboration not only enriches scientific inquiries but also fosters the creative spirit necessary to explore ideas that exist at the fringes of comprehension.

As we push forward into this speculative domain, we must also plant the seeds for the next generation of scientists who will embrace the challenges and possibilities that tachyon research presents. Educating aspiring physicists and researchers to explore the intricacies of tachyons requires robust educational frameworks that emphasize both theoretical foundations and practical applications. By crafting curricula that integrate core scientific principles with opportunities for inquiry into superluminal particles, educational institutions can inspire young minds to engage with the complexities of modern physics.

Encouraging critical thinking, creativity, and interdisciplinary exploration will be key components in preparing future scientists to address the fundamental questions that arise from tachyon studies. Research programs, mentorship opportunities, and outreach initiatives focused on tachyon dynamics could empower students to actively participate in the scientific discourse, ultimately cultivating a workforce passionate about the pursuit of knowledge and discovery.

Moreover, fostering environments that celebrate curiosity and challenge paradigms will unlock new avenues for potential breakthroughs. Future scientists equipped with knowledge about tachyons and their implications may contribute to advancements across various fields, from fundamental physics to applied technologies. These innovators will help shape the next frontier of scientific exploration, bridging the gap between theoretical research and transformative applications that redefine our understanding of existence.

In conclusion, the exploration of tachyons holds tremendous promise for redefining existing branches of science while simultaneously catalyzing the education of the next generation of scientists. By embracing the speculative nature of tachyon research, we open doors to new paradigms of understanding in physics and inspire future learners to engage with the complexities of the universe. As we inch forward into this uncharted territory, the potential for discovery fueled by tachyon dynamics propels us toward a future filled with hope, curiosity, and the boundless desire to unveil the underlying mysteries of existence.

11.5. Next Generation of Scientists

As we venture deeper into the realm of tachyon studies, it becomes abundantly clear that the next generation of scientists will play a pivotal role in shaping our understanding of these hypothetical particles and their implications. Cultivating an environment steeped in curiosity and interdisciplinary exploration is crucial for fostering advancements in tachyon research. In this context, educational pathways that inspire young minds to engage with the complexities of particle physics and theoretical inquiry will illuminate future avenues of scientific discovery.

To effectively educate the next generation of scientists, we must first establish foundational curricula that encompass both theoretical frameworks and practical applications related to tachyons and superluminal dynamics. This training should not only provide an in-depth understanding of existing scientific principles but also encourage students to explore the rich tapestry of ideas surrounding time, causality, and the very fabric of the universe. Courses that integrate advanced mathematics, quantum mechanics, and relativity with emphasis on speculative theories will empower students to navigate the intricate connections between established science and innovative inquiry.

Interdisciplinary collaboration will prove essential as students seek to bridge the chasms between various fields of study. Integrating knowledge from physics, philosophy, and engineering allows for holistic interpretations of tachyon dynamics, spurring critical discussions around their potential impacts on technology and society. By encouraging interactions among disciplines, educational institutions can cultivate environments where creativity and scientific rigor converge, enabling young scientists to approach their inquiries with fresh perspectives.

As part of this initiative, mentorship programs should be established to connect aspiring researchers with experienced scientists engaged in tachyon studies. Guidance from established scholars will provide invaluable insights into navigating the complexities of research, while also emphasizing the importance of ethical considerations and responsible scientific practice. Through these mentorship relationships, students can gain exposure to cutting-edge research, fostering excitement and commitment to expanding the boundaries of knowledge.

Moreover, the integration of modern technology—like online learning platforms and virtual collaborations—can enhance access to resources and education for students around the globe. By leveraging the power of digital tools, young scientists can participate in global dialogues surrounding tachyon research, engage with expert talks, and collaborate on projects transcending geographical barriers. This democratization of knowledge will stimulate an inclusive scientific community that mirrors the interconnected nature of the universe itself.

In tandem with educational initiatives, outreach programs should work to inspire curiosity among younger audiences through science communication campaigns. Engaging storytelling about the potential of tachyons—coupled with interactive experiences like workshops or exhibitions—will foster an early appreciation for scientific inquiry. By demystifying complex concepts and showcasing the impact of tachyon research, these efforts can sow the seeds of interest in fields related to physics and engineering.

As students embark on their educational journey centered on tachyons, it is imperative to remind them of the value of skepticism in scientific inquiry. Challenging assumptions, critically evaluating hypotheses, and diligently pursuing empirical evidence remain essential components of the scientific method. Nurturing an environment that promotes critical thinking lays the groundwork for responsible and innovative researchers who will contribute to the ongoing discourse surrounding tachyons and their far-reaching implications.

Ultimately, the next generation of scientists holds immense potential to illuminate the complexities of tachyon research and its myriad applications. By equipping aspiring researchers with the knowledge, skills, and tools needed to explore these frontier ideas, we set the stage for groundbreaking advancements that may redefine our understanding of time and space. As they delve into the exciting realm of tachyons, today's students could become tomorrow's pioneers—pushing the boundaries of human knowledge and unraveling the mysteries that lie at the heart of existence. It is our duty to inspire, educate, and empower them, ensuring that the journey into the world of tachyons is one of curiosity, innovation, and profound discovery.